WISDOM

AND THE MILLERS

Proverbs for Children

23,000 copies in print

Mildred A. Martin

WISDOM

AND THE MILLERS

by Mildred A. Martin

Green Pastures Press

7102 Lynn Rd.
Minerva, OH 44657

ISBN 0-9627643-0-2

Printed in U S A

Table of Contents

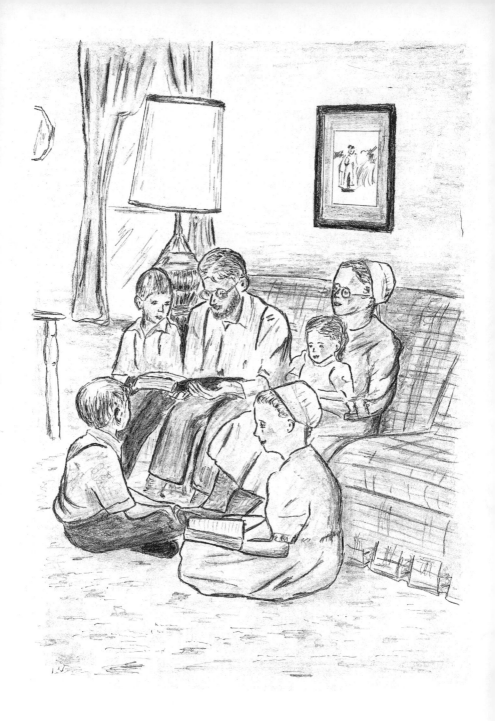

1

DISCRETION

Proverbs 3:21-23

It was evening, and the Miller family was having their devotions. Mom Miller sat on the couch with little Laura on her lap. Timmy and Sharon sat beside her, and Peter was on the floor at her feet. Dad had his big Bible opened to the book of Proverbs for the third night in a row.

"We're ready for chapter three," he announced, and began to read aloud: "My son, forget not my law; but let thine heart keep my commandments . . . "

Eight-year old Peter listened carefully. He liked the book of Proverbs. It was interesting, and he always wanted to know what the big words meant. "Dad," he interrupted suddenly, "What is *discretion*?"

"Discretion means being careful," his father replied. "It means thinking ahead to

what might happen, before you do something."
He went back to verse 21, and read it again:
". . . keep sound wisdom and discretion: so
shall they be life unto thy soul, and grace
to thy neck. Then shalt thou walk in thy
way safely, and thy foot shall not stumble."

"Discretion will keep us safe from most
trouble," Dad explained.

"That sounds like you today, Peter," said
big sister Sharon, with a teasing grin. "If
you would have thought about what might
happen before you played that noisy game
beside the beehive, you wouldn't have that
big swollen lump beside your eye! You didn't
have discretion, so you got stung!"

"*You* needed discretion today, too!" Peter
flashed back. "If you hadn't poured that
hot water into the sink on top of the dishes,
you wouldn't have broken that good drinking
glass!"

"All right," Dad smiled, holding up his
hand to prevent further argument. "Everyone
makes mistakes sometimes, through a lack
of discretion. We all need to learn to think
ahead before we decide to do something.
And that reminds me of a story . . ."

All the children's eyes turned expectantly
toward him, as Dad continued: "When I
was a little boy, my school teacher told our
class that we were supposed to make a bird's
nest for a science project. I guess she wanted
us to learn that God has given little birds

8

the skill to do something that people can't possibly do as well! But we second graders were sure, at first, that it would be an easy job. I secretly decided that I was going to make the best birds' nest in the whole classroom!

"While walking home from school that day, I planned how my nest would be made. I was going to use pine needles from our woods, and a little string here and there to hold it together . . . But when our neighbor's dog came running out to meet me, as she usually did, I suddenly had an idea how I could improve my nest! The neighbor's dog was a beautiful collie named Lady, with soft gold-and-white fur. She was a friend of mine, and came eagerly when I called. I opened my lunch box and took out the crust of peanut-butter sandwich which I had left, and then I took out the little scissors from my book-bag pocket."

"Oh, no!" exclaimed Peter softly. "Did you really cut off the dog's fur, Dad?"

"Yes, Peter," Dad went on sorrowfully, but with a twinkle in his eye. "While Lady finished my sandwich, I took my scissors and snipped off a nice little pile of golden fur from the ruff around her neck. Then I gathered it all up and trotted home."

"What happened next?" Timmy asked breathlessly. "Well," Dad finished, "our neighbor man was very angry. He had always

9

been so proud of his beautiful collie dog, and in two thoughtless minutes I had ruined her looks. It was almost a year before the fur grew back the way it had been. Your grandpa spanked me for purposely damaging another person's property, and my birds' nest didn't turn out all that well anyway. After we took them to school to show the teacher, I threw mine away as soon as possible. I felt too embarrassed every time I looked at it because it made me remember how foolish I had been."

"So, what does discretion mean? Dad asked the children again. "Being wise and thinking ahead," answered Sharon soberly.

"Let's pray for discretion; not only to keep out of danger, but also to keep away from evil!" Dad Miller said.

2

THE FROWARD MOUTH

Proverbs 4:24

The Miller family was gathered again for their evening devotions. Tonight Dad turned to the fourth chapter of Proverbs. "Hear, ye children, the instruction of a father, and attend to know understanding," he read. He paused, and Timmy wiggled a little as they waited for him to continue. "You see, children," he explained, looking around at each young Miller, "Children have many lessons to learn in life, and if you always obey your parents and teachers, you can learn your lessons the easy way. If you don't listen, but rebel, then life will teach you the lessons in a harder way."

Dad read on, until he came to verse 24: "Put away from thee a froward mouth, and perverse lips put far from thee."

"What does that verse mean?" Peter asked curiously.

Dad thought for a minute. "Froward means stubborn," he decided. "And perverse means . . . well, like ornery or contrary. A person who has a froward mouth and perverse lips is someone who argues and talks back." He looked meaningfully at little Laura, and she turned to hide her face in Mom's shoulder, embarrassed. Just a bit earlier that evening, Mom had asked Laura to pick up some toys, and Laura had answered defiantly, "*Mommy* pick them up!" So Mom had had to spank her, to teach her not to talk back to her parents.

Now Dad smiled reassuringly at his little two-year-old daughter. "We will try to teach you, Laura, while you're young," he promised, "so that you will not grow up to have a froward mouth and perverse lips. If children are allowed to talk back to their parents when they are small, they will grow up with a habit of arguing that is difficult to break. Then someday their big talk will get them into big trouble."

"That reminds me of a boy I knew when I was a girl in school," Mom spoke up. "I think we were in the sixth grade . . . " and sixth grader Sharon leaned forward expectantly to listen.

"You don't need to know this boy''s name," Mom went on, "so we will just call him John.

"Now John had a very froward and perverse mouth; he wanted to argue about almost everything. If the teacher wanted us to use pencils, he would raise his hand and say that he couldn't see why he shouldn't use a pen. If the teacher said we were to play kickball, John would gripe that he wanted to play softball. The teacher punished him different times for his disrespect, but he would always argue again.

"Then one day toward the end of the year, our teacher took us on a field trip. It was a beautiful spring day, and we were all so excited! We went in a big van, and took our lunches along. I don't remember exactly what kind of factory it was that we were taken to see, but it was some kind of food-manufacturing place. We left our van in the big parking lot and walked into a reception room, where one of the factory managers met us to guide our tour. John was arguing again that day, as usual; he didn't want to stand in line, and he kept touching things that the Teacher had told him to leave alone. He wanted to go look for a pop machine, and when Teacher told him to wait until after the tour, he said angrily, 'You mean a fellow can't even get a drink?' Even the factory people looked at John disapprovingly, and we all felt a little embarrassed.

"Then the factory manager brought out a box, and opened it. Inside were white paper hats, paper shoes, and little white paper masks to cover our mouths. 'The state laws require all visitors to wear these when they go through our factory,' he explained, and began passing them out to us children. We giggled and put them on. . . all except John. 'No way!' he said loudly. '*I'm* not gonna wear that stupid stuff!'

"There was a moment of horrified silence. Then the factory manager frowned at John. 'I guess I'm not going to take you along on the tour, then,' he said deliberately. 'A boy who won't do as he is told would be too big a risk. You might mess around with some of our machines, and be injured.' He turned to our teacher. 'Is it okay with you if we leave him right here until we are done? The secretary can watch him.'

"Teacher agreed, and so John was left behind the big desk, on a hard wooden chair, beside a stern-looking woman.

"And there he sat, red-faced and silent, as the rest of us walked away for our tour. John's froward mouth had brought him terrible shame, and caused him to miss the treats that we others had that day."

Mom was silent, remembering, and Peter sighed. "I sure wouldn't want anything like that to happen to me!" he said softly. "Put

away from thee a froward mouth, and perverse
lips put far from thee."

3

GO TO THE ANT

Proverbs 6:6-8

Peter, Timmy, and Sharon Miller sat on the shady porch steps, unhappily eyeing the bushel basket of green beans that was before them. "*Such* a lot of beans -- I guess there's a trillion billion in that basket!" moaned 5-year-old Timmy.

"We won't be able to get done before supper time," Peter grumped. "We'll have to work all afternoon, with no time to play."

"Come on, then, get started," Sharon said briskly. "See, I have a lot in my pan already."

Peter grudgingly picked out a long green bean. "Get busy, Timmy!" he ordered. "You slowpoke, you haven't even done one!"

"Slowpoke, yourself," replied Timmy, trying to make his voice sound deep like Dad's. "*You* get busy first, and then I will."

"You boys quit that fussing and work," said Sharon. "I'm soon going to quit working and rest until you start!"

Mom heard the commotion, and came out to the porch. "Children," she told them quietly, "Don't you remember the proverbs we read last night, the ones about the ant?"

"Yes! Go to the ant, thou sluggard, and learn to work!" Sharon volunteered. "These boys are being sluggards."

The corners of Mom's mouth twitched. "That wasn't all it said about the ant," she told the children. "Here, I'll get the Bible and show you." Mom quickly found the sixth chapter of Proverbs, and read aloud: "Go to the ant, thou sluggard; consider her ways and be wise: which having no guide, overseer or ruler, provideth her meat in the summer and gathereth her food in the harvest."

"You see," she explained, "it says that the ants have no boss or overseer to keep them at their work. Each one just keeps on working steadily by herself, without stopping to boss another ant. God made the ants to work in the summertime, providing a store of food for the winter; and He planned for us to do the same thing. These beans you are snapping now will be food for us in the winter."

Mom bent to look closely at the cement walk. "See there?" she exclaimed softly. The children looked where she was pointing, and saw a little black ant, carrying in his jaws a crumb of bread about twice its size. "Why, he's crawling backwards!" Peter noticed. "Yes," said Mom, "that crumb is so heavy for him that he must crawl backwards and drag it along. Yet he doesn't complain that it's too big a job!"

The four Millers watched the ant as it continued slowly across the cement: over a crack and around a stick, always dragging the load without stopping to rest. Finally it reached the grass at the edge, where another ant suddenly appeared to help with the burden. In a minute the ants and their crumb were out of sight among the grass.

"No one told those ants that they had to work," Mom told the children. "They don't boss each other around, not one word! Each one just goes out and works faithfully without being reminded.

"Now," she smiled. "I want you three to consider the ants and to work just like them. Each of you keep *yourself* at your work, and work steadily like that little ant!"

Mom returned to her work in the house, and the three children applied the lesson that they had learned from the ants; so well, in fact, that they were done early enough to have some time to play before supper!

4

REBUKE A WISE MAN, AND HE WILL LOVE THEE

Proverbs 9:8

Tonight the Miller family was studying the ninth chapter of Proverbs. "This chapter is all about wisdom, and how to be wise," Dad told his family. "Verse ten tells us where we can find the very beginning of wisdom: by knowing what God wants of us, and trying to please Him. 'The *fear of the Lord* is the beginning of wisdom,'" he read aloud with emphasis, "'and the *knowledge of the Holy* is understanding.'"

"Now," Dad said, "I want you to especially notice verse 8. Peter, you read it again for us, please."

Peter's brown finger moved rapidly up and down the page in his own Bible, until he found it: "Reprove not a scorner, lest he hate thee; rebuke a wise man, and he will love thee."

"What does that mean, Daddy?" Timmy asked curiously.

"Well," Dad replied, "those two words 'reprove' and 'rebuke' mean about the same thing. When I reprove you, I tell you about something that you are doing wrong. 'Rebuke' means to criticize or scold. We all need to be reproved and rebuked sometimes when we are not doing what we should be! But this verse shows the difference between the wise person and the foolish one. A foolish person is a scorner, who hates the one that rebukes him; while the wise man takes reproof with a good attitude, and loves the one who has shown him where he was wrong."

"I want to tell you two stories from the Bible," Dad went on, "that show what happened when the wise and the foolish were rebuked." He paged back through his Bible to the Book of Numbers. "Both of these stories are about people who made the same mistake: they had a rebellious attitude toward Moses, the leader God had chosen. First, I will tell you what happened to Korah, Dathan, and Abiram."

"Oh, I remember that one!" Timmy whispered. His eyes were round as he thought of the dreadful things that had happened in that story.

"Yes," Dad said. "You've heard this story before. But it's very important to learn the lesson it teaches. Korah and his friends, Dathan and Abiram, were men who thought their leader took too much on himself. That means they thought he was too bossy, and they didn't like to submit and obey quietly. So, they gathered together against Moses and said, 'What makes you think you should tell us what to do? We are all God's holy people!' Now, Moses really wasn't proud or bossy at all. When they spoke to him like that, he didn't get angry; he just fell on his face before the Lord, and humbly asked Him to show who was to be the leader of the people. Then Moses very kindly rebuked Korah and his men for their rebellious attitude, and told them to come before the Lord to see the sign that He would show them.

"But Dathan and Abiram answered, 'You just want to make yourself a prince over us! We will not come up!' They were scorners, you see, who hated to be rebuked; just like our verse from Proverbs tonight. And whenever anyone refuses to hear reproof, they are putting themselves in danger of worse punishment.

"The Lord spoke to Moses, saying, 'Tell all the congregation to stand far away from the tents of Korah and Dathan and Abiram, for I am going to punish them.' So all the people moved back from around the tents of the rebellious men, just in time; for as soon as Moses finished speaking, there was a great earthquake! The ground cracked open under the feet of Korah and Dathan and Abiram, and these men who had defied their leader fell down alive into the pit. The Bible says that the earth closed upon them and swallowed them up, with everything that belonged to them, and they were never seen again. What a terrible punishment! But it shows what God thinks of those who are rebellious and will not hear rebuke."

"What's the second story?" Sharon asked. "Is it about Aaron and Miriam?"

"That's right!" Dad replied approvingly. "Aaron the priest and Miriam the prophetess were the older brother and sister of Moses. But it was still wrong for them to speak against him the way they did. They were scornful of the Ethiopean woman whom he had married, and they said: 'What's so great about Moses? The Lord speaks through us, too!' Now the Bible says that God heard this, and his anger was kindled against them. Since they were also leaders of the people, they should have been more careful to set a good example! God spoke suddenly to Moses, Aaron, and Miriam, telling them to come into the tabernacle.

"There the Lord came down in the pillar of cloud, and He spoke directly to Aaron and

Miriam, rebuking them for their disrespect. When the cloud departed from the tabernacle, they looked at Miriam--and behold, she had turned white with leprosy! But Aaron and Miriam were wise enough to take their reproof the right way. They admitted that they had done wrong. Aaron confessed his sin, humbly asking Moses to forgive them and heal Miriam. So Moses cried unto the Lord, and Miriam was healed! You can be sure that Aaron and Miriam learned their lesson, and didn't do the same thing again."

"All of us can choose," Mom spoke up, "whether to be wise or to be foolish. At home or at school, when parents or teachers need to rebuke children, you can tell which ones are wise and which children are not wise. The foolish children will pout and say things like this: 'She's always picking on me!', 'Our teacher is so bossy!', 'He's always telling me to be more careful!' They feel rebellious, and do not try to obey; so usually they go on to get themselves in worse trouble.

But wise children will accept reproof quietly, and apologize for what they have done. They will love their parents and teachers even more, for showing them how to do better. I hope that you children will always be among the wise ones!"

"I be wise, too," little Laura declared solemnly, and the others smiled.

5

THE MULTITUDE OF WORDS

Proverbs 10:19

Sharon Miller had a problem. It was a lovely Fall day with multi-colored trees against the deepest of blue skies, but Sharon was too miserable to notice. Her head hung dejectedly as she shuffled slowly home from school. Peter had galloped on ahead, so there was no one to see when a tear dripped from one cheek to land in the fallen leaves. Today had been a terrible day for Sharon -- and she knew all too well that it was her own fault!

As soon as Sharon walked in the door at home, her mother knew that something was wrong. Wisely, she waited until a moment when she could be alone with her

daughter, and then she asked, "Sharon, what's the matter? You seem so sad this evening."

"Oh, Mom!" Sharon burst out. "Why do I always say such dumb things? I'm always getting in trouble for saying things I shouldn't, and today was the worst of all!" "Let's sit over here, and you can tell me about it," Mom replied gravely.

Sitting on the couch with her mother, Sharon poured out the sad story. "First of all," she began slowly, "this morning Martha Yoder told me what a pretty dress I was wearing." And I said, 'Oh, this thing is as old as the hills. It's almost ready to patch here on the sleeve, and then I'm going to throw it away! I'd *never* wear patches to school!' Just then I noticed Marie standing there listening. She was wearing her blue dress with two little patches on it! I know they are poor, and I would never want to hurt her feelings, because she's my best friend! But she felt bad about what I said, and she would barely talk to me the rest of the day.

"Then at noon, when my class was walking up to the ball field, talking and laughing, suddenly everyone was quiet. I wanted to say something, so I told a silly joke -- real loud. Nobody laughed, and one of the ninth grade boys shoved me and whispered, 'Don't be so dumb, Sharon! That was *really* inconsiderate!' Then I looked around and saw why everyone else had been quiet. We were just walking past the lower graders, who were all sitting in a circle on the grass, praying. I was *so* embarrassed, Mom!"

"And at the last recess," Sharon continued, "I was teasing one of the older girls about a boy. I know we aren't allowed to do that. This was the first time I ever did. But I wanted something to say, and it just slipped out. Somehow, Brother Ken heard me, and he sent me back to the classroom to sit alone until recess was over. Mom, I wish I didn't have to go back to school tomorrow! Why do I always say such dumb things?"

Mom put her arm around Sharon. "You do have a problem, Sharon," she said soberly. "But I think you understand yourself what the problem is, so you should be able to overcome it."

"What do you mean, Mom?"

"Well, in these sad stories from today, you mentioned the same thing several times," Mom replied. "You said, 'I guess I wanted to have something to say!' And I believe *that* is your problem. Too often, you try to think of something smart to say, when it would be better not to say anything at all. Sharon, you've always been a big talker, ever since you were a baby!" Mom sat remembering and smiled to herself. "You started to say words before you could walk, and by the time you were two, you could say anything. When you were older, you jabbered all the time, so that Dad and I often had to tell you to be quiet. We had a hard time training you not to use idle words, like 'oh, man!' or 'that's crazy!' or 'shoot!' Now it seems like you still have to struggle with the problem of talking too much."

"This morning when Martha politely admired your dress, you should have politely answered, 'Thank you.' Just a simple 'thank you' would have been the proper thing to say. But when you tried to think of a smart remark, you got into trouble and offended your friend. And all the other times, you made trouble for yourself by talking when you should have been silent. You will have to learn this rule, Sharon: *it is always wiser to say nothing when you don't know what to say.*"

Mom reached for the Bible on the end table beside them and turned to Proverbs. "Here is the chapter we are going to read tonight, and it has just the verse you need," she said. "Verse nineteen tells us: 'In the multitude of words there wanteth not sin: but he that refraineth his lips is wise.' *Wanteth* here in this text means 'lacking' or 'missing'. When a person talks too much, using a multitude of words, sin is never missing! The person who talks just to be talking is liable to sin by using idle words, boasting, stretching the truth, or offending others with fooolishness. A wise person will keep quiet until he has something valuable to say. Do you understand, Sharon?"

Sharon sighed and nodded. "Yes, I'll just have to try not to talk so much," she said softly. "I'm sure that's what I need to do, so I don't ever have another awful day like today!"

That evening as Dad Miller read again from Proverbs: "In the multitude of words there wanteth not sin, but he that refraineth his lips is wise," Sharon smiled knowingly at her mother. She was sure that *she* wanted to be among the wise!

6

AS SMOKE TO THE EYES

Proverbs 10:26

The Miller family was having a very busy day. Dad had just plowed the garden, and Mom wanted to get the spring vegetables planted while the ground was dry. Also, there was another exciting reason why they had to hurry: Uncle Steve's from Virginia were coming to Grandpa's for a week-end visit!

While the Millers ate a quick early supper, Mom and Dad planned their evening. "We only have the onions, potatoes, and carrots to plant yet," said Mom, "and that shouldn't take more than an hour or two."

"So we should be able to get cleaned up

and leave by seven-thirty?" Dad questioned.

"To go to Grandpa's house!" Timmy cried.

"And then we can see Uncle Steve's and the cousins!" Peter chimed in happily.

"But we will have to hurry," Dad warned. "If it takes too long to get the garden in, we will have to wait until tomorrow to go over to Grandpa's."

Peter looked down at his plate. He didn't like the word "hurry" when it was connected with work! Peter was never a slowpoke when there were games to be played. He was a fast runner, and a quick thinker. But it seemed like Dad and Mom were always telling him to hurry up when there was work to do. "Guess I'll *have* to hurry tonight," Peter thought grudgingly. He sure didn't want to wait until tomorrow to play with the cousins from Virginia!

After supper, Sharon stayed in the house to do the dishes, while the rest of the Millers trooped back outside. Dad started up the tiller and Mom began pounding a stake to make the first row of onions. "Peter, run and get me the biggest hoe from the garage," she directed.

Peter set out for the garage, but he didn't run. His tummy was full of supper, and he didn't feel like running. He grasped the hoe handle and lifted it carefully down from the high place where it hung. The heavy hoe swayed in his hand, and that gave Peter an idea. "I wonder if I can balance it, standing up in my hand?" he thought to himself. Putting the very end of the handle upright in his palm, Peter tried to keep it standing straight. For an instant he could, but then . . . CRASH! The heavy hoe teetered and toppled down, narrowly missing the family car! Guiltily, Peter picked up the hoe and trotted out of the garage, just as he heard Mom call, "Peter! Where's the hoe? I'm waiting for it!"

When Mom had made the row, she gave Peter a bag of tiny onion sets to plant. "Put them about this far apart," she showed him, "and then I will cover them when you have the row all done." She sent Timmy and little Laura to gather sticks for marking the carrot rows, then took up the rake and began smoothing the soil in the carrot bed.

Peter planted onions briskly for a few minutes, but soon decided that it was a boring job. "I wish I could do something exciting," he thought, "like running the tiller!" Setting down his bag of onions, he leaped across the rows over to where Dad was tilling. "Dad, can I run the tiller for a little?" he shouted above the noise of the motor.

Dad frowned slightly. "Aren't you supposed to be doing something else?" he inquired. "Go finish the job Mom told you to do, and then ask her if you may."

Disappointed, Peter plodded slowly back to the other side of the garden. A big earthworm slithered away from his foot, and Peter bent over and seized it. "I know what I'll do," he thought. "I'll catch a whole bunch of worms and put them in the onion row to turn the soil!" He looked over at Mom, made sure she wasn't watching him, and then went running to find an empty tin can.

When Mom finished planting carrots, she looked around. Where was Peter? Had he finished the onions yet? A quick look showed her that he had not gone even a quarter of the way down the long row. "Peter, where are you?" Mom called. There was no answer, and she raised her voice, "Pe-ter!" Still no reply, and Mom sent Timmy to look for his brother. Then she trudged down the onion row and began planting the rest of the sets herself.

When Timmy finally found Peter, he was still on the back porch where he had gone to look for a tin can . . . but now he had forgotten all about worms and was digging through a box of old tools. "Peter!" Timmy panted, "Mom wants you to come right away! Remember we have to hurry, so we can go to Grandpa's."

Peter remembered, and he hastily returned to the garden. "Peter, where have you been when you're supposed to be working?" Mom asked. She was not happy with him at all.

"It's getting late, and we still have the potatoes to do! Go quickly to the kitchen now, and bring me the old paring knife," she went on, "but don't run when you are carrying the knife!"

Peter sighed and headed back to the house once more. "I'm so tired," he thought to himself, forgetting that he had not actually done much work. His steps slowed as he passed the sandbox, where Laura was now playing, and his thoughts became grumpier yet: "I wish I was only two, then I wouldn't have to work so hard!"

The kitchen was empty when Peter entered, for Sharon had finished and gone out to help. First Peter got himself a drink, then he opened the kitchen drawer to rummage around for the knife that Mom wanted. Suddenly, he thought about the new pocket-knife that Grandpa had given him for his birthday. "I want to take my knife along to school on Monday for show and tell," he decided, "so I'd better go put it in my bookbag right now!" And with that, Peter went galloping upstairs.

Meanwhile, out at the garden, Mom had prepared the three double potato rows for planting, but Peter still had not returned with the knife to cut up the seed potatoes. "Sharon, you go bring me a knife," she said. "I don't know where Peter is, and we can't wait any longer!"

Dad had put away the tiller, and he joined Mom at the potato patch. "Aren't the potatoes done yet?" he asked in surprise. He pulled out his watch from his pants pocket. "Quarter after scvcn already," he stated. "I'm afraid . . ." he didn't finish, but bent over and began cutting up potatoes with the knife Sharon brought.

After awhile Peter came hurrying guiltily out to the garden too, and picked up a hoe. He began smoothing dirt over the potatoes, working silently as if he hoped no one would notice him. But dusk was falling by the time the last potato piece was covered. Dad pulled out his watch again. "It's after eight," he said softly. "By the time we would wash up a little and drive over to Grandpa's it will be nine o'clock. It's not worth going over tonight anymore!"

He looked at Mom, and she nodded sadly. "I guess we'd better wait until tomorrow," she agreed.

"Can't we go to Grandpa's?" little Laura asked. A big tear began to roll down her cheek.

"It's all Peter's fault!" Timmy cried. "He kept poking around and slowing us down!"

Dad was looking at Peter, too. "Son, you come with me," he said. "We need to have a talk." Peter's heart was full of dread as he followed his father. Was Dad going to punish him?

"Peter," Dad began soberly when they were alone, "you were very undependable tonight. You were slow to obey, and slow to bring the things you were sent for. You didn't do your share of the work, and that made it harder for everyone else. When you can't be depended on to obey quickly, you are a hindrance instead of a help."

Peter looked down at his shoes. He knew his father was right. "Have you ever had smoke in your eyes?" Dad asked next.

Peter looked up in surprise. "Yes, I'm sure I have," he replied, wondering what Dad was getting at.

"And do you remember how your teeth feel when you suck on a lemon or eat sour pickles?" Peter nodded, grimacing.

"There is a verse in tonight's chapter of Proverbs, which talks about smoke in the eyes and sour vinegar," Dad said. He reached for his Bible, opened it at the marker, and read: "As vinegar to the teeth, and as smoke to the eyes, so is the sluggard to them that send him" (Proverbs 10:26). Smoke in the eyes is bothersome, and annoying, and painful," Dad explained. "And that's just how you made Mom feel when she sent you to bring things quickly, but you made her wait and wait! You are being a sluggard, when you don't obey promptly."

"Now, Peter," Dad finished, "I want you to memorize this verse. Then, if you are wise, you will try very hard to form the habit of obeying quickly!"

"Yes, Dad, I will try," Peter promised. He repeated the verse to himself: "As vinegar to the teeth, and as smoke to the eyes, so is the sluggard to them that send him."

7

A TALEBEARER

Proverbs 11:13

The eleventh chapter of Proverbs was a long one, so Dad decided to read only half of it in an evening. "We will read down to verse fourteen now," he told the family, "and tomorrow night we can study the other half."

Dad and Mom and Sharon and Peter took turns reading the verses carefully and clearly. "Now I want you to notice two of these verses especially," Dad said when they had finished. "Verse twelve: 'He that is void of wisdom despiseth his neighbor, but a man of understanding holdeth his peace.' And verse thirteen: 'A talebearer revealeth secrets; but he that is of a faithful spirit concealeth the matter.'"

43

"These verses," Dad explained, "teach us about the wise man's attitude toward others. A foolish person feels proud, and thinks that he is better than others. He also enjoys talking about others in unkind ways. But those who are wise, are always humble! A wise person will not tattle or gossip about others, because he has the proper respect for everyone."

Dad turned to his younger son. "Timmy," he said, "can you tell us what the word 'tale-bearer' means?"

Timmy thought hard, but then shrugged. "I don't know," he admitted.

"I do!" Peter answered eagerly. "A tale-bearer is a tattle-tale!"

"That's right, Peter," Dad replied. "A tale-bearer can be a tattle-tale, or a gossiper, and also a person who tells someone else's secrets. Now, children," Dad continued, "I'll tell you a story to illustrate this. When I was a boy . . . " he paused, with a faraway look as he remembered.

"Oh, goody!" whispered Timmy, bouncing a little in his seat. "A story about when Daddy was a little boy!"

"When I was about your age, Timmy, or a bit older," Dad went on, "I had a bad habit of tale-bearing. I was a big tattle-tale, always running to my parents to tell them about every little thing that I thought my brothers were doing wrong. And I always tried hard

44

to be the first to tell any interesting piece of news, whether or not it was something I was supposed to tell. My parents tried to help me stop being such a tattler, but it seemed like I would never learn! Then one day something happened which made me realize how hurtful a talebearer can be.

"My Grandpa had asked to have one of us boys to help him for the day, and our parents decided that my brother Ben should go. Ben was two years older than me, and I thought he looked so big and important as he climbed into Grandpa's car. They drove out the lane together, and were gone all day.

"As suppertime neared, I hung around in the front yard, watching eagerly for Grandpa's car. At last he came! Grandpa was in a hurry, so he just dropped Ben off and drove away. Ben came running up to meet me. 'Look what I have!' he said importantly. He reached in his pocket and slowly pulled out -- a dollar bill! My eyes grew round with wonder.

"'I picked up rocks out of Grandpa's garden all day, and put them on a pile,' Ben told me happily. 'And then Grandpa paid me this! It's the first dollar I ever earned. I'm going to tell Mom, and surprise her!' Ben turned toward the house.

"But now I saw *my* chance to tell something really exciting. 'I'm going to tell her first!' I shouted, and began to run.

'No, no, don't!' Ben cried desperately. "'It's mine, and I want to surprise Mom!' I paid no attention. He ran after me, but I was a fast runner, and Ben was worn out from his day's work. I burst into the house ahead of him, determined to be the first with this big news.

"Mother was at the sink, and I grabbed her skirt. 'Mom!' I gasped out, 'Grandpa paid Ben -- a whole dollar bill!' And I turned to grin triumphantly at Ben, who was just coming in the door.

"Then the grin froze on my face, and my stomach felt like doing a flip-flop. Ben was crying! My big, strong eight-year-old brother was crying like a baby. I had spoiled his big surprise, and he was heartbroken. He ran to Mom and sobbed out his disappointment in her arms. Mom tried to comfort him, and I put my arms around him too. 'I'm sorry, Ben,' I said contritely. My selfish, thoughtless talebearing had hurt my brother very much. For the first time I understood why it was not always good to tell everything I knew.

"Probably my habit wasn't broken all in one day, but that was the turning point. I learned to think, before I told something interesting: 'Is this really true? is it kind? Will it hurt someone's feelings, or spoil a surprise?' Each of you children must remember to ask yourself these questions too. A wise person knows whcn to 'hold his peace.'

"Let's repeat verse thirteen together," Dad finished. "A talebearer revealeth secrets; but he that is of a faithful spirit concealeth the matter."

8

HE THAT WATERETH

Proverbs 11:24,25

"Me have some! Peter, give me some!" Laura danced around eagerly when she saw what Peter was taking out of his bookbag along with his homework. It was a whole roll of lifesavers, and the Miller children didn't get candy very often.

But Peter turned away from his little sister's pleading eyes and outstretched fingers. "No, Laura," he growled. "I'm not going to open these now. I got them for a prize in school, and I'm going to save them!" In a low voice he added, "Then sometime I'm going to eat them all by myself."

He didn't mean for anyone else to hear that last part; but Mom had sharp ears, and she looked sadly at Peter. "Put those away, and come for devotions now," she told him.

The family gathered at the couch, and Dad began reading the second half of Proverbs eleven. "Notice verses 24 and 25," he said when they were finished. He read them again: "There is that scattereth, and yet increaseth; and there is that withholdeth more than is meet, yet it tendeth to poverty. The liberal soul shall be made fat, and he that watereth shall be watered also himself."

"These verses mean," Dad explained, "that a generous person who shares with others, often ends up having more than the selfish person who tries to keep everything for himself. This is a hard thing for some people to understand, especially children. They think that the best way to be happy and to have enough is to keep everything they can! But God has planned that those who share will be blessed the most."

Peter squirmed. That roll of life-savers felt hard and uncomfortable in his back pocket. Did Dad know about them?

But no one seemed to be looking at Peter. "Do you know any stories about people like that?" Timmy asked hopefully. It was always nice to have Mom or Dad's stories to illustrate Bible verses!

Mom smiled at Dad and nodded. "When I was a little girl in Costa Rica," she began, "my grandparents once came down on an airplane to visit us. It was the first time we had seen them for several years, and we were all so excited! Of course, they had presents for all of us. And they even brought each of us children a big Hershey chocolate bar! That was a real treat, because we didn't have Hershey bars in Costa Rica. All my little brothers and sisters gobbled theirs up the first day, and then felt rather sick afterwards. But I and my sister Mandie were more prudent: we each took little nibbles from one corner of our Hershey bars, and then put them away to save for later. I was determined that I would enjoy mine for a long, long time!

"Grandpa's visited us for a week, and we were all rather sad and lonely the day they left. But as we children were wandering around grumpily that evening, not sure what to do next, Mandie had an idea for cheering us up! She went to her desk drawer and brought out her precious Hershey bar. Returning to the kitchen, she took a knife and divided the chocolate into little squares. Then she passed them out to everyone, a piece for each -- even me! She ate just one of the little pieces herself, and beamed so happily at everyone else's happiness. Mandie always did love to share! There was just one piece left after she had given everybody one, and she wrapped it up to put back into her drawer. But the very next day when one of the little boys fell and cut his leg, I saw her giving him that last piece to stop his tears.

"Now Mandie's Hershey bar was all gone! She didn't seem to mind a bit. Mine was safe in my drawer, and I didn't plan on wasting any of it. I thought Mandie was silly, to give most of hers away. Every once in awhile I would go and check if my chocolate was still there. I would sniff the rich delicious smell, but I didn't eat any. 'Some day,' I promised myself. On a very special day I would get out that Hershey bar and eat it all by myself!

"At last the day came, when I decided to eat my chocolate bar. I waited until no one else was looking, and crept cautiously into the bedroom. It had been several days since I last looked at the candy, so now I opened the drawer with eager anticipation. I reached down under the pile of things where I'd hidden it, and grasped the paper wrapper.

"But what was this? The brown paper and foil were empty! Well, almost empty. A swarm of tiny sugar-ants hurried away from my hand. They had been busy with the candy: there was only a little bit of sticky, chewed chocolate left!

"Tears of disappointment stung my eyes. My long-awaited treat was ruined! But I wept alone. I was ashamed to tell any of the others what had happened to my hoarded

Hershey bar. They might have said that it served me right!"

"Maybe it did serve you right," Dad chuckled. Mom laughed too.

"That's not the end of the story, though," she went on, looking at her eager listeners. "The next time my father went to town, I saw my Mother whisper something to him. He smiled, and whispered a reply.

"Then when he came home, he smiled an even bigger smile as he pulled a little paper bag out of his pocket. 'Here, Mandie,' he said as he handed it to her. 'You shared your candy with everyone, so we are giving you some more!' And there was a whole handful of chocolate candies in that bag. But can you guess what Mandie did with them?"

"She shared those, too!" the Miller children chorused.

"That's right," Mom replied. "She had learned the lesson of our verses from Proverbs tonight."

"The liberal soul shall be made fat, and he that watereth shall be watered also himself," Dad quoted once more. And Peter resolved in his heart that as soon as devotions were over, he was going to give everybody one of his lifesavers!

9

THE RIGHTEOUS MAN'S BEAST

Proverbs 12:10

"Dad, may we have devotions out on the porch tonight?" Sharon begged. "It's so hot this evening!"

"Well, that sounds like a good idea," replied Dad Miller. "Timmy, you may bring the Bible." And the Millers all trooped out to the slightly cooler porch.

For awhile they sang, joining their voices with the crickets and other creatures in the summer evening's chorus. Then Dad opened the Bible to Proverbs twelve. We will take the first ten verses tonight," he said, and began to read by the fading light of the setting sun. At verse ten he paused. "This is the verse I want you children to learn tonight," he told them. "'A righteous man regardeth the life of his beast: but the tender mercies of the wicked are cruel.'"

"Shall I tell you about how my father taught me the truth of this verse?" Dad asked, smiling. He knew what their answer would be.

"Oh, yes, Dad!" "Tell us!" cried the children eagerly.

"Well, when I was about Peter's age," Dad began, "my father went to a minister's meeting a hundred miles away from home. He was going to be gone overnight, and come back the following afternoon. It was my brother Ben's turn to go along, so I was going to be the oldest boy at home! Dad gave me instructions on how to take care of things while he was gone. 'You can do the chores,' he told me. 'Milk the nanny goat, and be careful to keep the milk clean. Don't forget to give the goats and chickens feed and water twice a day. And be sure to help your mother with whatever you can!' I assured him that I would be able to handle everything, and so they left.

"That evening I felt very important and responsible as I went out to feed the animals. I did the chickens first, since they were the easiest. Next I went to take care of the goats, and to milk Nanny. It looked so easy when Dad did it! He would have the pan brimful

56

of foamy milk in just a few minutes, with Nanny standing quietly throughout. But she didn't always behave so well for me!

I gave the young goats their feed dishes outside of the pen, so they wouldn't get in the way. Next I filled Nanny's dish extra full, hoping to keep her still while I milked; and nervously approached the big goat. She rolled her eyes at me, as if disapproving of this little fellow who was trying to take her master's place; but then she settled down and began crunching feed. I milked as fast as I could, racing to finish before the goat finished her feed, but it was hard work. My small hands got tired, and I would have to stop and rest every now and then. The pan was barely half full when she licked up the last crumb of grain and turned to stare at me.

"Quick as lightning, one hind leg jerked up, and -- Splash! she plunged her hoof right into the pan of milk. 'You dumb goat!' I screamed. I knew better than to kick her, but I certainly felt like it. The way Nanny looked at me with those yellow eyes made me sure that she had done it on purpose! Now I would have to pour the milk out on the ground, because I knew Mom would never use it.

Sadly I gathered up the milk pan and feed dishes. I checked the goat's water bucket, noticing that there was still about an inch of water left. 'I don't feel like getting them more water now,' I growled to myself. 'It's so far to carry the bucket. And serves Nanny right if she gets thirsty before morning!'

"The next morning the milking went better. Nanny ate her feed more slowly, and I managed to get through before she did. Feeling happy and successful, I whistled as I carried the milk to the house. But I completely forgot to look at the water bucket, so I didn't see that the goats had already licked it dry!

"That day the goats seemed more noisy than usual. 'Ba-a-a-a-a!' they bleated. 'Ba-a-a-a-a!' over and over. 'Why do the goats keep crying?' Mom wondered. 'Peter, please go and check.'

"I trotted out to the pasture and peeked over the fence. 'Ba-a-a-a-a!' they cried when they saw me, but I couldn't see anything wrong. They're just "ba-ing" because they're lonely for Dad,' I reported, and my mother laughed.

"But the goats kept bleating all day, and by the time Dad returned in the afternoon, their voices sounded very hoarse. A chorus of pitiful 'Ba-a-a-a's met Dad as he stepped out of his car. 'What's the matter, girl?' he asked, scratching around Nanny's horns. And then he saw the empty water buckets!

"I don't remember very often that I saw my father angry, but he was angry with me that day. 'Didn't you give them any water this morning?' he asked sternly. I admitted that I had forgotten. 'What about last night?' Guiltily I admitted that I hadn't given them any then, either. 'So they have been without water all day in this heat?' I kept my eyes on the ground, where my bare feet were nervously scuffing the dust, and nodded.

"'Peter, look at me,' my father commanded, and I obeyed. 'You were responsible to take care of these animals. The Bible says that a righteous man regardeth the life of his beast. It is not right to let our animals suffer neglect or cruelty. Peter, when did *you* last take a drink?' Startled, I tried to remember. 'It must have been at lunchtime,' I replied, 'because I'm thirsty now.'

"'Well, Peter,' he told me gravely, 'here's what your punishment will be. For the rest of the day you will not be allowed to drink anything. You may go without water yourself until tomorrow morning. That way you should never again forget to give water to the animals in your care.'

"Did you get very thirsty, Dad?" Peter asked softly, thinking of that long-ago boy who was also named Peter.

"Yes, I did," Dad replied. "There was no glass of water at my place on the supper table, and no drink at bedtime. It was hard for me to fall asleep that night, because I was so thirsty. But my father was right --

that lesson stuck with me for the rest of my life. I always think of it when I read this verse: 'A righteous man regardeth the life of his beast, but the tender mercies of the wicked are cruel.'"

10

THE LIP OF TRUTH

Proverbs 12:19,22

Timmy Miller would not be going to school until next year, but he liked to make art projects just like the school children did. Right now he was sitting at the table with his paintbrush and watercolors, painting a motto on a piece of roofing slate which Dad had given him. Timmy had great hopes for this motto. It was going to be the prettiest thing he had ever made!

He had painted a woodland scene on the slate, with green pine trees and a sun and blue sky. There were even some little red flowers. Now, Timmy wanted to paint some words to a very short verse. "Mom," he asked, "how do you spell 'God is Love'?"

Slowly, one letter at a time, Mom spelled the verse. Timmy painted each letter as neatly as he could. At last the motto was done! Timmy felt so happy as he held it up for his mother to admire. "It's beautiful, Timmy!" Mom encouraged. "You did a very good job of painting and lettering. Now we must put it in a safe place to dry, until after supper." She helped him set it on the buffet in the living room, at a spot where it should not get bumped.

"Now let's go set the table for supper!" Mom said.

All through the meal that evening, Timmy kept thinking about his motto. As soon as he could, he excused himself from the table and went to fetch it. Eagerly, he reached up to lift it from its perch on the buffet, anticipating how he would show it to Dad and the others.

But then the family sitting in the kitchen heard a wail of disappointment. "It's ruined!" Timmy cried, bursting into the kitchen with his motto. "Somebody smeared the letters all up!"

"Who could have done that?" Mom wondered sadly. She turned and looked at the most likely culprit, who was sitting in her high chair with guilt written plainly on her face. "Laura, did you smear Timmy's picture?" Mom asked sternly.

The little girl's lip quivered, and a big fat

tear spilled from one eye; but she nodded her head. "Y-y-yes," she answered tremblingly.

"Well, Laura, we are glad that you told the truth," Mom said, putting an arm around her. "It would have much worse if you had lied. Since you told the truth about it, I guess we won't spank you this time."

Dad lifted Timmy onto his lap. "I think we can fix your motto," he consoled his son. "We can wash the paint off here where it's smeared and do the lettering again."

Later the family turned in their Bibles to Proverbs twelve, and read verses eleven to twenty-eight. "Many of these verses speak about truth and lies," Dad commented. "Verse thirteen: 'The wicked is snared by the transgression of his lips.' That's talking about how liars get themselves into trouble. Often people think that if they tell a lie, when the truth doesn't seem to be convenient, they can save themselves trouble. But it doesn't work that way!

"If Laura would have lied about smearing Timmy's motto," he went on, smiling at his youngest daughter, "she would have been spanked for lying. Telling the truth set her free.

"Verse seventeen tells us: 'He that speaketh truth showeth forth righteousness, but a false witness deceit. And verse nineteen: 'The lip of truth shall be established forever; but a lying tongue is but for a moment.'

"Children, I want to tell you a story to illustrate that last verse," Dad told them. "When I was a schoolboy, our reader had a story about a boy named George Washington. The story told how he had a little hatchet, and wanted to chop something with it. Foolishly, he chopped down a small tree which his father had planted on their farm: a cherry tree!

"Of course, when his father saw the ruined tree, there was trouble. 'Who chopped down my cherry tree?' Mr. Washington inquired sternly.

"Little George was probably very much afraid. Perhaps his first thought was to lie, and try to save himself from punishment. But the story says that he confessed to his father: 'I cannot tell a lie. I did it, with my little hatchet!'

"Peter," Dad questioned, "can you tell us what George Washington grew up to be?"

"The first President of our country," Peter replied.

"That's right," said Dad. "And this little story of how he told the truth has been repeated over and over for hundreds of years. Thousands of parents have told the story to their children, and millions of American boys and girls have read about it in school. 'The lip of truth shall be established forever,' the Bible says, 'but a lying tongue is but for a moment.' If young George Washington would have lied about that cherry tree, his words would not have been established nor remembered. He would have been punished, and the incident soon forgotten. We would not remember him now, hundreds of years later, for telling the truth."

"And if he had grown up to be a liar, he wouldn't have gotten to be President, either, would he?" Sharon stated.

"Probably not," Dad smiled. "But the most important reason why we should not lie is in verse twenty-two. Let's read it together.

"'Lying lips are abomination to the Lord, but they that deal truly are His delight,'" the family read aloud.

"The most important reason why we must tell the truth is, that it pleases God," Dad explained. "Lying lips are an abomination to Him, which means that He hates them very much. We all want to please the Lord more than anything, and one way to do that is by always telling the truth."

11

A COMPANION OF FOOLS

Proverbs 13:20

Soft lamplight glowed in the living room, touching the contented faces of the Millers. What better place to be on a chilly wet evening like this, than the warm family circle with a Bible at the center?

"Proverbs thirteen tells us about some of the laws of life," Dad was saying. "There are natural laws, like the law of gravity: whatever goes up must come down. If you throw a stone into the air, it will come down again. If you jump out of a window, without anything to catch you, you will fall until you hit the ground. The law of gravity is the same for everyone, and man cannot change it. Verse thirteen is like that; it is a law that God has set up, and man cannot change it." He read, "'Whoso despiseth the Word [of God] shall be destroyed; but he that feareth the commandment shall be rewarded.'"

"And verse twenty is another one: 'He that walketh with wise men shall be wise, but a companion of fools shall be destroyed.' These are God's laws of life, and they always hold true. Some people think that they can break these laws and get away with it. 'It doesn't mean me,' they think; or, '*I'm* strong enough to go with bad company and not be harmed.' But God's spiritual laws are as fixed as the laws of gravity, and what He says will come to pass. God's law says that if you spend your time with wise people, you will become wise. And if you spend your time with fools and ungodly people, you will be destroyed."

Mom arose from her seat and crossed the room, coming back with an object in her hand. "Do you see this wooden stool, children?" she said. "I am going to tell you the story of the boy who made it for me."

The Miller children looked wonderingly at the small brightly painted stool. It had been part of their living room furniture for as long as they could remember, and they had never thought to ask where it had come from!

"When I was teaching school years ago in another state," Mom began, "there was a boy in my class named Jake. He was the kind of boy everybody likes: pleasant and cheerful, a good student, a hard worker, and a good ballplayer. He was strong and healthy and good-looking, and he seemed able to do a good job at whatever he tried. He was only about eight years old when he made this stool, and brought it as a present for the teacher. You can see what a skillful piece of work it is, for an eight-year-old!

It appeared that God had blessed Jake, with many talents and skills. Everyone expected that he would grow up to be a good worker for the Lord.

"When Jake was about fifteen, though, he began to spend a lot of time with ungodly young boys; boys who had not had Christian training. He developed close friendships with these fellows, and would sneak away from home to meet with them against his parents' wishes.

"Of course, when he was with them, he tried all the forbidden things that they offered. He tasted whiskey, and tried cigarettes, and used tobacco and beer. He really didn't enjoy such things at first, but he felt pressured to do whatever his friends did; so, he kept on trying until he became used to them. His ungodly friends also liked to roar around the countryside on motorcycles, filling the emptiness in their lives with a lot of speed and noise. So, Jake learned to drive a motorcycle, too.

"His parents and church friends tried to warn him about the danger of what he was doing, but Jake would not listen. He only laughed at their concern. 'I'm strong and smart and careful,' he would say. 'I can have a little fun, and it won't hurt me. I will settle down and become a Christian someday, when I'm ready!'"

"But that day never came for Jake. One night as he was speeding down some back country roads on a motorcycle with his rough friends, there was an accident. Jake was thrown from his motorcycle and killed suddenly -- too suddenly to have any chance for prayer or repentance. Jake was hurled into eternity without Jesus, lost forever. His bright, talented young life was wasted.

"Jake had liked to say, 'Nothing will ever happen to *me*!' But he was wrong, just as people are always wrong when they doubt the truth of God's Word. The Bible tells us that a companion of fools will be destroyed, and that was exactly what happened.

"Children," Mom finished soberly. "I want this wooden stool to be a reminder to you. Every time you see it, remember that the warnings and promises in God's Word are true. If you are ever tempted to play with sin, and think that it won't harm you, remember Jake."

71

"We want to always choose wise people for our friends," Dad added. "It is one of God's laws of life, that you become like the people you are with. That's why it is so important to choose friends carefully. 'He that walketh with wise men shall be wise, but a companion of fools shall be destroyed.'"

12

MAKING MOCK AT SIN

Proverbs 14:9, 16

It was a rainy Saturday afternoon, and the Miller children were running out of things to do. They had been busy helping Mom with housework most of the morning, but now their playtime was hanging heavy on their hands. Sharon had drifted off to lie across her bed with a book, and the boys weren't quite sure what to do next.

"Let's play Pick-Up-Stix," Timmy suggested.

"No! I'm tired of that," Peter sighed. He picked up a little toy car and began pushing it aimlessly around on the carpet.

"I know, let's have a wreck!" Timmy giggled. He picked up another little car and

sent it flying across the floor. Crack! It slammed right into Peter's car, and both vehicles tipped over on their sides. Anxiously, Peter picked up the little cars to see if they had been hurt, but the "accident" had left no marks.

"All right, Timmy!" he exclaimed. "Get out all our little cars, and we'll play highway!" The boys had a dozen or more little cars, and the long, curving stripes on Mom's braided rug made perfect highway lanes. They zoomed the little cars around and around, making sure to have a "wreck" every so often. Then Peter had another idea to add to the excitement!

"I'm a drunk driver," he told Timmy in a low voice, feeling sure that this was not something he wanted his parents to hear. "See my car weave around?" And he made the little car rock and tip as it careened crazily down the highway. Crash! There was another wreck, the biggest one yet. Cars went spinning in all directions! Peter and Timmy forgot about keeping quiet, and roared with laughter.

"Here goes the drunk man!" Timmy cried, staggering around the room.

"I can't walk in a straight line!" Peter gasped. He lifted an imaginary bottle to his lips for another "drink", then wobbled harder until he dropped to the floor with a heavy thump.

"You're terribly drunk, Peter!" Timmy whooped.

Suddenly Dad was standing in the living room door. "What do you boys think you are doing? he asked. His voice was quiet, but stern. Poor Peter and Timmy would rather have crawled under the big braided rug, than to face that look of disappointment in his eyes.

"We were playing with our cars, and . . . " Peter faltered, "and then we . . . we played that we were drunk."

For a long moment there was silence, as Dad looked at the guilty faces of his sons. "Do you think that was a wise thing to play, boys?" he spoke at last. Shamefacedly, they shook their heads.

Dad put an arm around each boy and led them over to the couch, where he seated them on his knees. "Boys," he told them soberly, "real drunk drivers kill many people every day. They cause a lot of pain and suffering, and a lot of blood and tears. They hurt real children just like you, and fathers like me. That's not anything to laugh and joke about."

Peter hung his head, and Timmy picked nervously at his sleeve. "The Bible has a verse about laughing at sin," Dad went on. "Right in Proverbs, chapter fourteen. He reached for his Bible, and read: "'Fools make a mock at sin, but among the righteous there is favor'."

"Do you boys want to be fools?" Dad asked.

"Oh, no, Dad!" Peter answered, and Timmy shook his head vigorously.

"I'm sure you don't want to be fools," Dad told them, with a smile and a hug. "So, I'm telling you what the Bible says about how to be wise. If the Bible says that fools make a mock at sin, you know that you don't want to do such a thing again. Verse sixteen of the same chapter says, 'A wise man feareth, and departeth from evil.' Wise people know the seriousness of sin. They fear to displease the Lord, so they will not touch sin, even in play.

"If we make a mock of sin, that shows we don't think it is as serious as we should," Dad told his sons soberly. "We show ourselves to be foolish, if we ever pretend to be doing something that is wrong. That includes pretending to kill others, or pretending to smoke or drink, or pretending to steal. So you can see why we don't allow you to play games like 'cops and robbers'."

"Dad," Peter remarked thoughtfully, "one of the neighbor boys had some candy once that looked like cigarettes. He offered me one, but I didn't take it because I thought it would be wrong."

"You were right, Peter!" Dad answered with approval. "It would have been foolish

77

to play smoking with candy cigarettes. The Bible tells us to avoid all appearance of evil. Also that would have been another example of making mock at sin."

He stood up. "Well, boys, I think I know what your problem was today. You didn't have enough to do, and so you got into trouble. Am I right?" The boys looked sheepish. They could guess what was coming next!

"You may put on your boots and go down to the basement now," Dad directed. There's still quite a stack of those boards with nails in them. Pull out all the nails, and then pile the boards up with the firewood. If you keep at it, you can be done by suppertime."

Peter and Timmy went slowly down the basement stairs with their hammers. Pulling nails was a job they didn't enjoy, but it was still better than a spanking! They felt sure that they would never again want to make a mock at sin.

13

A PLACE OF REFUGE

Proverbs 14:26

"'In the fear of the Lord is strong confidence,'" Dad Miller read aloud, "'and His children shall have a place of refuge.' Proverbs fourteen twenty-six."

Dad looked around at his family, sitting in the cozy circle of lamplight. "Here is one of the many Bible verses which tell us about God's care and protection," he told them. "Christians are very safe and secure. When we are following God's will for our lives, we are in the safest possible place to be; even though there are dangers all around. God has all power to keep us from any harm that He does not want us to experience. Can you children think of any other Bible verses that talk about His protection?"

"The Angel of the Lord encampeth round about them that fear Him, and delivereth them," Sharon quoted.

"I will trust and not be afraid," Timmy addcd, rcmembering a Bible School verse.

"The Lord is good, a stronghold in the day of trouble," Peter said, thinking of a chorus they had sung in school that day.

"Do you have any story tonight to go with our theme?" Dad asked, turning to Mom with a smile.

"Yes," she replied, "these verses remind me of a story I read in a newsletter a couple of years ago.

"On a dark night in Africa," she began, "a man named Benson Bichaba was creeping silently up to a little house. Benson was a thief, who stole whatever he could from other people's houses. He had a heavy smoking habit, and was always needing more money to buy cigarettes. Tonight he had chosen this house at the edge of a village, to steal from. Cautiously he crept behind some bushes, where he could look into a window and wait until the people in thc housc wcnt to bed."

Timmy looked at the dark windows of his own living room, and a cold shiver went up his back bone. What if there would be a stranger out there right now, watching him and planning to come in and steal? "Mom, I don't like such a scary story!' he said uneasily.

81

"It's all right, Timmy," Mom reassured him. "Wait till you hear what happened!" She put a comforting arm around him, and went on.

"But the family living in this house were Christians, and they were gathered together for prayer before they went to bed. They knelt in the little room, lighted by a single candle, as their father prayed for safety through the night. Outside in the bushes, the listening thief could hear every word. As the praying father finished, he said something that struck terror into the sinful heart of Benson Bichaba!

"'Lord, I pray that You will send away the thief that is outside,' he said in a strong confident voice, 'and thank You for protecting us tonight! In Jesus' Name, Amen.'

"Benson Bichaba didn't dare to linger a moment longer by that house! Tremblingly, he slunk away among the bushes. As soon as he thought he was out of earshot, he began to run in wild panic. All he could think of was getting far away from that house with the praying man. 'How did he know? How did that man know I was outside?' He gasped as he ran. When he could go no farther, he collapsed on the ground sobbing for breath.

"At last his panic subsided, and Benson began to think. 'I must find out more about this Lord Jesus,' he decided. Rising up, he returned to the village, to a home where he knew that a Christian minister lived. Meekly, he knocked on the door, and asked to speak to the man of God.

"The hour was getting late, but the minister was still glad to help a lost soul find the Lord. For a long time he spoke with Benson, explaining about God's way of salvation. And that night Benson Bichaba became a Christian believer!

"Before he left the minister's house, Benson still wanted to have an answer to his question: 'How did that man know there was a thief outside?'

"The old minister thought for a moment. 'Well,' he told Benson at last, 'it's possible that he saw you. But more likely the Lord led that father to pray as he did, for the safety of his family. God didn't want you to steal tonight, Benson; He wanted you to find salvation instead.'"

Timmy glanced again at the dark windows on the other side of the room. Somehow they didn't look so scary now! He joined in heartily with his family as they repeated Proverbs 14:26 . . . "In the fear of the Lord is strong confidence; and His children shall find a place of refuge."

14

A SOFT ANSWER

Proverbs 15:1

The older Miller children were at school, and Laura and Timmy were playing together in the living room. Timmy was building a cabin with Lincoln Logs, while little Laura had been struggling for several minutes to build a block tower. It took a lot of effort and concentration for her little fat fingers to pile up more than a few without letting them fall. Carefully, she set on another block . . . then one more. The tower teetered a bit, but stayed upright.

"Timmy, look!" she crowed triumphantly. "I maked a big stack! One - two - three - four - five - six - seven blocks!"

Timmy laid down the log he was just ready to use, and turned around to see. But as he was turning, his sleeve brushed the top of the fragile block tower. Crash! The blocks all came tumbling down, and Laura let out a wail of disappointment. "You bad boy, Timmy!" she cried. Her blue eyes clouded with the sudden anger of the very young, and she jumped to her feet huffing and puffing with wrath. Her chubby fists were all ready to beat upon her brother. Only quick action could save Timmy now!

Ducking away from her threatening blows, he said quickly, "I'm sorry, Laura! I didn't mean to wreck it. I'll build you a bigger one right away, with ten blocks!"

The anger faded from Laura's face as suddenly as it had come, and she sat down with a thump. "Okay, Timmy!" she told him eagerly. "Ten blocks!"

Mom had hurried in from the kitchen, just in time to see Timmy head off the threatened fight. Quietly, she watched as Timmy constructed the promised ten-block tower, and admired it when it was done. Then she called the children over to sit on the couch with her.

"Timmy," she said lovingly, "you were very wise to be a peacemaker, and avoid trouble like that. The Bible says that a soft answer turneth away wrath, and that's what you did: you turned away Laura's anger and saved both of you from a nasty fight."

"But, Laura," Mom went on, "you must not get so angry. You are three years old now, a big girl. You must learn to control yourself and not be so easily upset."

That evening the very first verse Dad read in devotions was Proverbs 15:1 -- "A soft answer turneth away wrath, but grievous words stir up anger." Timmy's eyes lit up as he recognized the words. He grinned at Mom, and she smiled back.

"Children, let's think about this first verse," Dad said when he finished reading the passage he had chosen. "Verse one teaches us an important principle for getting along with other people. To live in peace, we need to be willing to give a soft answer.

"If we have offended someone, a soft and humble apology will usually make things right. When we have an argument or difference of opinion with someone, we also need to answer softly and humbly, even though we may be sure that we are right! People who are proud and stubborn will answer with grievous words, and that only makes the problem worse. Grievous words stir up anger.

"Your Grandpa likes to tell a story to illustrate this verse," Dad went on. "It happened one day when he was driving in another state, far from home. Darkness was falling, just as he entered the outskirts of a small town. Suddenly the red flashers of a police car flared up behind him! Grandpa was being stopped, and he didn't know why. Carefully, he pulled over to one side of the unfamiliar road, and shut off his engine. Nervously, he waited while the officer in the car behind him wrote down Grandpa's license number, and prepared his papers.

"At last the door of the patrol car opened, and out stepped the biggest, angriest-looking policeman Grandpa had ever seen! He stalked over to the window, and shining a flashlight into Grandpa's eyes, demanded to see his license. Politely, Grandpa handed him the card. The officer looked it over, and then angrily told Grandpa that he had been driving too fast. He swore, calling Grandpa a number of bad names, as he ranted about careless people who don't bother to obey the law. "You were going 35 miles an hour in a place where you should have gone 25!" he shouted. "Now, do you have any excuses?"

"A soft answer turneth away wrath . . . " the words flashed through Grandpa's mind. "No, I have no excuses," he answered humbly. "I must have been careless. I didn't see the 25 mph sign. I'm very sorry, and I will pay my fine."

"For a long moment, the angry officer stared at the meek face of the preacher. Then the anger faded from his eyes. He sighed, removed his hat and wiped the sweat from his forehead. "You'll have to excuse me for getting so worked up," he said in a calmer tone. "We've just had two wrecks here today, really bad ones. A drunk driver and some foolish kids, tearing around, with no respect for the law. Some innocent people were killed, and I'm still upset about it."

"He handed back Grandpa's license. "I can see you didn't intend to be speeding," he said, "so I won't give you a ticket. Drive carefully, now, and have a good trip!" and he waved Grandpa on.

"Grandpa often uses this incident for an example. How differently it could have turned out if he had argued or spoken rudely back to the officer! He would certainly have been forced to pay a fine, and might even have ended up in jail for resisting the law. Proverbs 15:1 is such an important verse! I want all you children to memorize it, if you haven't already."

"A soft answer turneth away wrath: but grievous words stir up anger."

15

TREASURE AND TROUBLE

Proverbs 15:16

There was great excitement in Sharon Miller's upper-grade classroom. This was the final week for Brother Ken's Health Habits chart, and there still remained several children who hadn't missed a square! Sharon was one of them, and she had high hopes of winning a prize.

The teacher had shown the prizes to his class. First Prize was a paintbox, the big kind that cost four dollars, with three brushes and lots of paints. That prize was only for the children who didn't miss one square on their charts. Then there would be brand new toothbrushes, in a variety of colors, for all those who missed less than three spaces.

The chart listed a lot of different health rules, and after three weeks most of the children had no hope of winning a paintbox. Sharon had been very careful, though, and so had her best friend Marie, as well as two of the ninth-graders. Until the very next to the last day!

Sharon was never quite sure afterward how it happened, but as she was standing before her chart on Thursday morning, coloring squares, it suddenly hit her! She gasped. Her face turned pale, then red, as the truth dawned. She had forgotten to brush her teeth before school that morning!

"Surely, I must have," Sharon thought desperately, but it was no use. Just running her tongue over her teeth proved that she had indeed forgotten.

Mechanically, Sharon kept on coloring spaces, just as if her day was not lying in ruins. "It isn't fair!" she mourned inwardly. "I was so careful! I made sure I slept 8 hours every night . . . and ate fruit every day . . . and washed my hands before every meal . . . and once I even went outside at bedtime to run around the house because I hadn't had my outdoor exercise that day . . . It isn't fair to lose my prize just because I forgot once!"

By the time Sharon had colored down to the square which said "Brush teeth every morning and evening", a tempting idea had popped into her mind. "I could just go to the restroom now and rinse my mouth really well," she thought, "and then tonight I would brush my teeth twice to make up for it!" Guiltily, Sharon looked around the classroom. No one seemed to be watching her, so she kept right on coloring. Her hand moved more slowly as she filled in that "toothbrushing" square, but she tried to convince herself that it was perfectly all right to do as she had planned.

There! Today's row was all done. There were still a few minutes left before first bell, so Sharon laid down her crayons and hurried to the restroom. At the sink, she bent over and rinsed her mouth for a long time. "Surely that's as good as brushing," she thought defensively.

But somehow, the day was spoiled for Sharon. The thought of what she had done kept coming back to haunt her. Each time she tried to justify herself, thinking of how much she deserved to win the first prize, and of how she would make it right. But the battle of conscience within her took the joy out of everything. "I'm not really being dishonest," she would argue; but her conscience told her otherwise.

Finally, that long, long school day came to an end, and Sharon could leave the classroom. Surely, when she could no longer see that accusing chart on the wall, she would forget! As soon as she reached home, Sharon went into the bathroom and locked the door. Then she brushed and brushed her teeth, more thoroughly than she had ever done in her life before. "Now you can quit worrying," she told herself. "I will be brushing my teeth twice today, so everything is all right!"

But Sharon was still miserable. That night as she sat with the family for devotions, her mind kept mulling over her problem. She wasn't paying much attention to the reading from Proverbs, until suddenly, one verse seemed to leap out at her.

"Better is little with the fear of the Lord, than great treasure and trouble therewith," Dad was reading aloud. Belatedly, Sharon glanced down at her own Bible, looking for the verse. There it was: Proverbs 15:16.

"Better is little with the fear of the Lord, than great treasure and trouble therewith!" Sharon knew exactly what that verse must mean. The 'great treasure' of the paintbox prize, which she so desperately wanted, was bringing her 'trouble therewith'. Wouldn't it be better to do what was right, even though she would have only a little toothbrush for a prize?

"I didn't do anything so wrong!" Sharon cried inwardly, but it was no use. "You weren't honest. You colored a square when you hadn't brushed your teeth," her conscience told her. Finally, before Sharon could go to sleep that night, she had to make up her mind. Tomorrow, she would go tell Brother Ken what she had done. She would have that one space empty on her chart, and take a toothbrush for her prize.

In the morning, Sharon was tempted to reconsider her decision, and the battle with herself had to be fought again. But it was much easier this time, as she remembered her misery the day before! Proverbs 15:16 was right. It wasn't worth being dishonest to get a paintbox . . . or any other treasure.

Sharon had a light heart as she went up to receive her new toothbrush. The verse she had learned in this time of trouble was ringing triumphantly in her ears: "Better is little with the fear of the Lord, than great treasure and trouble there with!"

16

PLEASANT WORDS

Proverbs 15:23

"My mind shall be God's workshop,
That every thought and word
And deed be kind and noble,
And honor Christ my Lord!"
the Millers were singing. All the Millers loved
to sing, from Dad down to little Laura. As
they finished the last line of "My Body is
God's Temple", both Peter and Timmy were
ready with more selections! But now Dad
shook his head. "It will soon be bedtime,"
he said regretfully, "so we'd better stop singing
for tonight. Let's turn to Proverbs fifteen,
and finish the chapter."

Beginning at verse 23, Dad read the last
eleven verses aloud.

"The theme we want to think about tonight," he told the family when he had finished, "is of wise speech and pleasant words. This passage has several verses that tell us how we should speak. Verse 26: "the words of the pure are pleasant words." And verse 28: 'The heart of the righteous studieth to answer, but the mouth of the wicked poureth out evil things." And verse 30: "A good report maketh the bones fat!" The children laughed at that last one.

"I want to especially think about verse 23," Dad went on. "A man hath joy by the answer of his mouth; and a word spoken in due season, how good is it!' When we speak kind words of encouragement to others, it makes them happy and gives us joy as well."

"A story!" said Timmy, hopefully, bouncing in his seat. "Do you know any story about kind words?"

"I'll tell you one," Mom answered with a smile. "It happened when I was a school girl, a little older than Sharon. Our church was having revival meetings, and on Friday morning the visiting minister came to school for devotions. The minister was a tall man with an enthusiastic style of speaking. He must have given us children an interesting talk that morning, but twenty years later, I have forgotten what it was about. I only remember what happened afterward.

"When the preacher had finished giving his talk, and closed with prayer, we children were dismissed to go to our classrooms. We had a large school, much bigger than the one you children attend, and there was a lot of bustle and noise as over a hundred children separated to file out for their first classes of the day. In the confusion, no one took time to speak to the visiting preacher! All at once I happened to look toward the back of the auditorium, and saw him standing there by himself. "Why, he looks kind of sad . . or lonely!" I realized. Perhaps he was discouraged that morning, or missed his own children far away.

"Impulsively I left the group of my classmates and headed for the other end of the room. The minister was just going through the doorway to the hall, and I hurried after him. Would I be in time? He took long steps, and I dared not run in the hallway. But I caught up, panting, just as he was going out the big double doors with no one to say goodbye. He noticed me and stopped, and I politely held out my hand.

"God bless you, Brother Harley," I said with a smile. "I appreciated your talk. Have a nice day!"

"That was all, but I felt good as I hurried back to my classroom. The preacher had looked happier as he left, and I wasn't even late for class!

"Many years passed before I met Brother Harley again. I was a grown woman the next time I shook his hand, but his face immediately lighted with recognition. "I know you!" he said. "You were the girl who cheered me up that day at your school. I was feeling very discouraged, and then you came running after me to say 'God bless you; have a nice day!' That encouraged me so much! I have never forgotten it."

"I hope you children never forget it either," Dad told them. "This was a perfect example of a good word spoken in due season. Do you see how even a child's words can bless and help a grown-up preacher? We should always be alert for a chance to encourage others, like your mother was. There is another verse in the Bible which tells us that "A word fitly spoken is like apples of gold in pictures of silver." Kind words are beautiful and precious."

"Is that verse in Proverbs too?" Peter wondered. "It sounds like a Proverb!"

"Yes, you are right," Mom answered laughing. "Proverbs 25:11."

"Let's say verse 23 together now, and try to remember to give pleasant words to others in due season," Dad concluded.

"A man hath joy by the answer of his mouth; and a word spoken in due season, how good is it!" The Millers repeated in unison.

17

BETTER THAN THE MIGHTY

Proverbs 16:32

"Daddy, see what I built?" Timmy stood at his father's elbow, holding out a little truck which he had put together from Lego blocks.

Dad looked up from the papers he was studying. "Why, that's very good, Timmy!" he encouraged. "What kind of truck is it?"

"It's a garbage truck!" Timmy replied, "and I'm pretending to . . . " he whirled around excitedly, ready to show Dad what he was playing.

Peter was on the floor too, building a fire

engine, and he had it almost done. But as Timmy turned, one of his feet came down a little too close to Peter's project. Snap! A clump of Lego pieces broke off and fell from the side of the fire truck.

"Timmy, look what you did!" Peter cried in despair. He jumped to his feet. His eyes were flashing with anger and one hand was raised, ready to slap his brother. But just as suddenly he let his hand fall to his side again. The fire faded from his eyes, as he made a visible effort to control his anger. Dropping to his knees, he began to gather up the pieces of his fire truck.

"I'm sorry, Peter," Timmy said softly. "I should have looked where I was stepping."

Dad rose up from the table, laid down his papers, and knelt beside Peter. "Here, let me help you put it back together," he offered. For a few minutes, father and son worked quietly together, repairing the little fire truck. When it was finished, and standing beside the little garbage truck all ready to go. Dad put an arm around his older son. "Peter," he said, "you showed yourself to have strong character just now, when you decided not to be angry."

Peter smiled sheepishly at his father. "I wanted to hit Timmy, but I knew that I shouldn't," he admitted.

"Remember last night's chapter of Proverbs?" Dad asked. "We read a verse there that talked about controlling our anger. Proverbs 16:32: 'He that is slow to anger is better than the mighty; and he that ruleth his spirit, than he that taketh a city'. This verse means that a person who can control himself and keep from showing anger, like you did now, is stronger than a mighty soldier who can conquer a city. Solomon knew how hard it is for people to rule their own spirits and exercise self control."

Dad seated himself and drew both sons close at his knees. "I'll tell you a story about this principle, from the life of David," he said. "Remember when David was just a boy, called to play on his harp and sing for King Saul? Saul was a mighty king, but he didn't have the strength of self-control. He threw his javelin at David in a jealous rage, trying to kill him. If David had not been a person of strong character, he might have picked up the javelin and thrown it back! Or he might have been angry and called Saul all kinds of bad names. But David was a man after God's own heart, and he was able to keep himself from foolish anger. He never lifted his hand to take any revenge against Saul, even though Saul spent years chasing and tormenting him.

"One night, after Saul and his soldiers had been hunting David through the wilderness all day, they camped out in a wild and lonely spot. David was in the mountains nearby, hiding from Saul; and he looked down and saw the camp of soldiers. He asked his friends, 'Who will go down with me to the camp?' and Abishai said, 'I will go with you.' So they crept quietly down the mountain together in the dark. When they reached Saul"s camp, they walked in among the sleeping soldiers without being discovered, for God had cast the army into a deep sleep. In the center of the camp, they found Saul himself lying asleep, with his weapons ready beside his pillow.

"Now, most people would have believed that David had a perfect right to kill Saul, after all that he had done to him. Even Abishai expected that this was what they had come for, and he made ready to drive his spear through Saul! But David stopped him. 'No,' he told Abishai, 'that is not what we're going to do. I will not lay my hand upon the Lord's annointed king, even though he doesn't please the Lord. Just take his spear and water bottle, so that we can prove we were here, and let's go.' Once again David showed that he could rule his own spirit, and keep himself from anger and revenge.

"Another time, when David was running from Absalom, a man named Shimei came out and followed after him, throwing stones and dust at him. He cursed David and called him ugly names. 'Shall we kill him?' David's men asked eagerly. But still David refused to get angry. 'Leave him alone,' he said meekly. 'Perhaps God has told him to curse me.' Later Shimei repented of what he had done, and came to apologize to David.

"These stories show us the great strength in David's character. Sometimes he needed to show righteous anger at sin, but he controlled his anger. He kept himself from hitting back at those who hurt him. David became a much mightier king than Saul, for Saul didn't have self-control. David was the most important king in all of Israel's history, the one who united his country and made it great.

"So, boys," Dad concluded. "You can see how important it is to have self-control. A boy who can rule his own spirit will be able to do great things for God! Those who can't, will not amount to much in life. We want to be slow to anger, like David. "He that is slow to anger is better than the mighty; and he that ruleth his own spirit, than he that taketh a city."

Dad returned to his papers, and Peter and Timmy went back to the model town they were building out of Lego blocks. But for a long time, the words of the Proverb kept ringing through Peter's head as he played: "He that is slow to anger is better than the mighty . . . better than the mighty."

18

A BROTHER'S LOVE

Proverbs 17:17

"Come for devotions!" Dad called, and all the children hurried to his side. "It's my turn for Dad's lap!" Timmy squealed happily.

Tonight the Millers were studying the second half of Proverbs 17. "The verse I want to talk about especially is verse 17," Dad told them when they had finished reading. "This verse tells us why God has given us friends, but especially brothers and sisters."

He repeated the verse: "A friend loveth at all times, and a brother is born for adversity." Sharon, can you tell us what 'adversity' means?"

"I guess it means hard times, or trouble," Sharon answered.

"That's exactly right," said Dad. "There's an old saying, which goes like this: 'A friend in need is a friend indeed.' A true friend will always help you in hard times or trouble. And God also made brothers and sisters to help each other when they need help. That is one reason why God planned for people to be born in families, so that they can love and help each other.

"God didn't plan for brothers and sisters to quarrel or fight with one another. But since sin came into the world, that is what they too often do," Dad went on sadly.

Peter and Timmy looked a bit guilty at that. "Is Dad thinking about how we were fighting before supper?" Peter wondered to himself.

"But that is not how God planned for brothers to be," Dad repeated, looking sternly at his sons as if he guessed their thoughts. "God wants brothers and sisters to love each other."

"Do you know any story about that?" Peter asked quickly.

"I do," Mom spoke up, "but it's a very sad story." The children listened soberly. "When I was Peter's age," Mom continued, "my family moved to Costa Rica, along with several other

Mennonite families, to start a mission church there. We had been living in our new home only about a month, when a volcano erupted!"

Peter and Sharon gasped. "A volcano," Mom explained to the little ones, "is a mountain that bursts open and explodes. Then fire and smoke come out, and sometimes a lot of people get killed. We don't have volcanoes around here," she added reassuringly.

"The Arenal volcano was an old one, and hadn't erupted for hundreds of years. People thought it was safe. But one day, without any warning, it exploded! Clouds of gray ashes fell like snow over the land, and hot poisonous gases hissed through the air, killing every person and animal who breathed them. My family lived far enough away from Arenal that we were in no danger, but many people had farms close around the volcano. The newspapers said that ninety-six people died from the poison gases and hot falling rocks.

"It was a very frightening time for us, who had just moved to a strange land," Mom told the children, "and there was a picture in the newspaper that I will never forget. It was a photo someone had taken of two dead boys, lying in their pasture, where they had gone to bring the cows home. They were about your size, Peter and Timmy, and they had been killed by the poisonous smoke.

But do you know why the newspaper men chose that picture to publish? They probably had many pictures of people killed by the volcano. But there was something special about that picture of two boys: it showed an example of brotherly love. The older boy was lying partly on top of the younger one, with his arms around his little brother. It looked like he had been trying to protect his brother from danger, even as he himself was dying." Mom's voice shook, and tears came to her eyes as she remembered.

"So, children," Dad finished gravely, "I hope that you will always remember this story, too. Those Costa Rican boys showed us a great example of the way God wants all brothers and sisters to love each other. He wants us to help one another, in good times and in times of trouble."

"A friend loveth at all times, and a brother is born for adversity."

19

FOLLY AND SHAME

Proverbs 18:13

"Laura, where did you get those stars?" big brother Peter demanded suspiciously.

"I got them for my birthday," little Laura replied quickly. She held the small paper of stickers behind her back, afraid that Peter would try to snatch them away.

"Let me see them," Peter said, taking a threatening step toward her. "I bet they are mine!"

Reluctantly, Laura held up the paper, keeping it clutched tight in both little fists. "Those look like mine!" Peter shouted. He hurried over to the dresser and opened the top drawer, where he kept his private possessions. After a hasty look, he shouted again, "Mine are gone! Laura, you took them! Give them right back!" He tried to grab the paper of stars and Laura began to scream.

"Whatever is the matter, children?" came their mother's voice from the doorway.

"He's taking my stars away!" Laura cried tearfully.

"But, Mom, they're mine! She took them out of my drawer," Peter accused.

"Peter, how could Laura open your drawer?" Mom asked calmly. "She isn't nearly tall enough. And she knows that you children aren't allowed to snoop in each other's drawers."

"She could have climbed on a chair," Peter answered stubbornly. "I know those stars are mine, because they look exactly like the ones I had. Laura doesn't have any of her own."

"Peter, you *don't* know that they are yours," Mom rebuked him. She sat down on the bed and lifted Laura onto her lap. Gently she took the little paper of stars from Laura's hand and turned it over. There on the back side was something that Peter hadn't seen! Written faintly in orange crayon were the words, "To Laura from her friend Ellen."

"See this, Peter?" Mom showed him. "I thought they were hers. Laura's little friend gave her these stars at church, for her birthday. Now I want you to go open your drawer again, and look more carefully for your own stars."

Silently Peter obeyed. The contents of his drawer were jumbled together in a rather disorderly way, and this time he rummaged around with his hands. It wasn't long before that paper of stars appeared, shining underneath a notebook. How they glittered and shone! And Peter's face shone, too, shiny red with embarassment.

"Peter, Peter," Mom spoke kindly. "See what shame you bring upon yourself, when you jump to conclusions? I hope you will never be so quick to accuse anyone again. Hasty accusations are always foolish. Now, I want you to tell Laura that you are sorry."

"I'm sorry, Laura," Peter said humbly.

"Now, Peter," said Mom, reaching for his Bible on the bed shelf, "tonight's chapter of Proverbs has a verse in it about jumping to conclusions. I want you to stay here in your room and read over chapter 18 until you find it. When you guess which verse it is, you may come and read it to me." Taking Laura by the hand, she walked away and left Peter alone.

A little while later, Peter came, with Bible in hand, to find his mother in the kitchen. "Some of these verses have such big words," he complained. "I'm not really sure which one it could be. But is it verse 13?"

"You guessed it!" Mom smiled. "That was hard because the verse doesn't say the words 'jumping to conclusions'. But you understood the sense of it, anyway. Read verse 13 aloud, Peter."

"He that answereth a matter before he heareth it, it is folly and shame unto him," Peter read.

"Yes, exactly," Mom replied. "It brings folly and shame upon us when we make hasty accusations, without hearing the facts. I want to tell you a story about this very same thing, but I will wait until this evening so that all the children can hear it."

That evening the Miller family took turns reading Proverbs 18, verse by verse. "What is the story you were going to tell, Mom?" Peter asked eagerly when they had finished.

"You have a story for one of these verses?" Dad questioned.

"Yes, verse 13," she replied.

"He that answereth a matter before he heareth it, it is folly and shame unto him," Dad read again. "Well, that sounds like it is talking about people who jump to conclusions."

"Right!" said Mom. "I want to tell a story about a boy who did just that, and falsely accused some innocent people.

"When I was a girl, I knew a boy who had a pet calf. The boy's name was Arnold; and he called his calf 'Hershey', because

116

its fur was the color of chocolate. Arnold had no other pets on his farm, and he was so fond of little Hershey! He even brought the calf to school when we had Pet Day. The teacher wouldn't let him bring such a big pet into the classroom, of course, but we all went outdoors to see Hershey and stroke his soft fur. Arnold took very good care of his precious calf, and Hershey grew strong and healthy. The rest of us children often listened as Arnold told all the latest about Hershey- how big he was getting and what a smart calf he was. When Arnold's parents invited my family over for dinner, we children went out to look at Hershey standing contentedly in his grassy field. As soon as Hershey saw Arnold, he came galloping over to the fence in hopes of finding a treat. He really was a beautiful calf!

"But one day Arnold was late for school. When he came in, the whole class could see that he had been crying. At recess time, we learned the terrible news. Hershey was gone! He had disappeared from his pasture during the night.

"'Whatever could have happened to him?' we demanded, shocked.

"'I don't know,' Arnold answered forlornly. 'Dad says someone may have stolen him. A nice calf like Hershey would bring a lot of money.' And his red eyes filled with tears again.

"We children stood around in little groups all recess, discussing the sad fate of poor Hershey. Nobody felt like playing, but we got a lot of talking done. John, a boy who was a big talker, soon had it all figured out. 'It stormed last night,' he told us, 'so the thieves came and got Hershey while the thunder was making so much noise. That way nobody could hear them. And I think I know who the thieves were, too!' he added importantly. Throwing a quick glance over his shoulder to make sure that the teacher was nowhere near, he went on, 'It was those neighbors of yours, Arnold. My Dad says they are a rough bunch, and maybe they sold Hershey to get money for more beer.'

"We all knew which neighbors he meant. The Smiths lived right next to Arnold's father's farm, and they were not Christians. Their yard looked like a junk pile, and they could often be heard shouting and swearing at one another. But would they steal a calf? John seemed convinced that they would, and the rest of us began to wonder.

"One evening John and a couple of his buddies decided to do a little detective work on their way home from school. They walked past the Smith's yard once, looking to see if anyone was home. Seeing no cars, they walked quietly in the lane. 'Look for clues!' John told them. 'Calf footprints, or rope, or whatever you can find.' They began to walk around the yard with their eyes on the ground, and didn't notice when Mrs. Smith appeared at a window. 'What are you boys doing?' she called suddenly. 'Did you lose something?'

"The three boys' heads went up like startled deer, and they dashed for the road. Only John, the boldest, had anything to say. 'Cattle thieves!' he shouted back as he ran! Mrs. Smith only looked puzzled as she closed her window again.

"The following week, Arnold's older brother was working on fences around their farm. He found a small break in one of the cow pasture fences, a place where the bottom wire had come loose from a post. While he was repairing the broken place, he kept noticing buzzards circling over at the edge of the woods nearby. So many buzzards were soaring, dipping, and landing that he finally became curious enough to go and see what they were eating. And there on the ground he found what remained of Arnold's pet calf!

"Even though the buzzards had been busy eating, Arnold's brother could still see a large black burned patch on the back of the dead calf. The night of the storm, poor Hershey must have panicked and broken through the weak place in the fence, to run for the shelter of the woods. On his way there, he had been struck by a bolt of lightening and killed. The mystery was solved!

"Now Arnold knew what had happened to Hershey, and he promptly told the news. All the boys who had been so sure that Smiths were the thieves, felt quite embarrassed. But worst of all was poor John. His father learned what he had done, and made him go to the Smiths and apologize. Imagine how awful he felt! Truly, jumping to conclusions had brought folly and shame. He had made up an answer for the matter before he heard the facts, and made a totally false accusation."

Thoughtfully, Peter and the rest of the Millers repeated Proverbs 18:13 together: "He that answereth a matter before he heareth it, it is folly and shame unto him."

20

ENVYING SINNERS

Proverbs 23:17

"Zoom -- zoom! Va - a - a - a - a - room."
A cloud of dust rose from the gravel road
as the three-wheeled motorbike roared by.

"There goes Mike Mayle again, with his
new three-wheeler!" Peter cried. He dashed
across the yard for a better look, with Timmy
and Laura close at his heels.

Mike, the sixteen-year-old neighbor boy,
sat straight and proud on the seat of his
new vehicle. He pretended not to notice
the Miller children watching. Gripping the
handlebars, he pulled back -- "Zip zoom!"
He popped a wheelie, nearly falling off, then
wobbled on down the road.

Peter doubled over with laughter. "Did
you see that silly Mike?" he gasped. And
Laura echoed, "Silly Mike!"

But Timmy stood silently watching as the three-wheeler disappeared down the road with its accompanying dust cloud. "I wish I could have a ride on that," he spoke finally. "Why can't we have a three-wheeler?"

"Because our church doesn't allow them!" Peter answered, shocked. "Anyway, they're dangerous. Don't you remember that magazine article Mom read to us? And they're a foolish waste of time, Dad said. Mike probably never does much work."

"Oh, don't be so bossy," Timmy answered in a grumpy tone. He turned and wandered slowly off across the yard with his head bent, kicking at grass clumps. The sunny summer day had lost its beauty for his eyes, as his heart filled with envy. "I don't care what they say," he thought rebelliously. "I wish we were allowed to have three-wheelers. We can't have anything that's exciting! I wish I was Mike, then I could go tearing around and not have to work on a nice day like this."

Peter was happily pushing Laura on their long rope swing, but Timmy didn't feel like playing. He leaned on the fence, peering down the road, hoping for another glimpse of the forbidden machine. "Zoom . . . zoom!" he muttered softly to himself. "Wish I could pop a wheelie!"

The envy in Timmy's heart spoiled his whole day. He was grouchy at lunchtime; and when it was time to work in the garden, he pouted and grumbled until Mom had to punish him. After that he felt a little better, but by suppertime he still had not forgotten about Mike and the three-wheeler.

As the Millers were eating supper, the phone rang. Mom went to answer it, and stood by the counter listening for a long time. "Oh, did they?" the family heard her say. "Well, that's too bad . . . yes, I guess so . . . Well . . . "

"It must be Mrs. Simmons," Sharon whispered to Peter. "She always wants to talk and talk about everything that's happening in the neighborhood!" Dad raised his hand in a "shh"ing gesture, and Sharon returned her attention to her bread and honey. But the food on Mom's plate was nearly cold before she hung up the phone and came back to the table.

"That was Mrs. Simmons," she told her family soberly. "She was telling me about an accident that happend today in the Mayle's field."

"What happened?" Dad inquired.

"Several boys were taking three-wheeler rides over the hill," Mom answered. "They had been drinking beer too, and it sounds like they were taking dares and showing off. There were two three-wheelers, and the boys drove them straight toward each other. There was a wreck, and Mike Mayle's vehicle tipped over on top of him. His right hand

124

was pinned underneath, and his fingers were mangled so badly that the doctors had to take three of them off. Another boy has a concussion, too."

Timmy sat staring into space, frozen with the shock of the news. His fist clenched around his spoon as his imagination vividly pictured those roaring motors . . and the terrible frightening crash. He thought of what it would feel like to have his hand crushed, and to have a doctor cutting his fingers off. He shuddered. How could Mike ever do anything now, with three fingers missing?

Suddenly Timmy didn't envy Mike anymore. He was glad to be himself, and have parents and ministers who saw the wisdom of forbidding such things as three-wheelers. Looking around at the peaceful kitchen and the faces of his family, Timmy felt safe and secure.

That night Dad read Proverbs 23 for devotions. Soon he came to some verses which seemed to be talking about Timmy's day!

"Let not thine heart envy sinners," Dad read, "but be thou in the fear of the Lord all day long. For surely there is an end, and thine expectation shall not be cut off. Hear thou, my son, and be wise; and guide thine heart in the way" (Proverbs 23:17-19).

"Children," Dad said gravely, "sin may sometimes look like a lot of fun. But we must be wise enough to consider the end of sinners. Sin is always punished sooner or later; if not in this life, then in the next. Even if drunk drivers don't have crashes, like Mike Mayle did this afternoon, they still will need to face the Lord someday. Even though drug dealers or thieves may not be caught by the police, they will still be punished in eternity if they do not repent.

"Whenever we are tempted to think that sin looks exciting, we must consider where that sin would lead us in the end . . and turn away from it. Let's not envy sinners! Sin isn't worth it."

Together the Millers repeated verse 17, and the words were especially meaningful for Timmy. "Let not thine heart envy sinners: but be thou in the fear of the Lord all the day long."

21

TAKING A DOG BY THE EARS

Proverbs 26:17

It was a sunny summer afternoon, and the Millers were enjoying a reunion with half a dozen families of their cousins. Two long tables stood in the yard, loaded with good things to eat. Dad, Grandpa, and the uncles were talking together in groups, while their wives sat visiting on lawn chairs. The children scattered here and there, playing games and getting better acquainted with cousins whom they seldom saw.

Suddenly the peaceful scene was broken by the sound of crying! All the mothers turned anxiously to see whether it was their own child they heard. Mom Miller jumped to her feet, for the children coming toward her were Peter and Timmy. Peter was leading a sobbing Timmy by the hand, and one hasty glance told which of them was hurt! Timmy's nose was bleeding, a crimson trickle of blood that dripped down his chin and over the front of his blue shirt.

Quick as a flash, Mom was at his side, with a paper napkin pressed to the streaming nose. "Tip your head back, Timmy," she ordered calmly, as she picked him up and started for the house.

Peter trotted alongside. "Mom, it was those big boys!" he fumed indignantly. "They were tussling in the back yard, and . . . "

"Just wait a minute," Mom told him quietly. "When we get inside you can tell me all about it."

In the kitchen, Mom got a cold wet washcloth for Timmy's nose, and the bleeding soon stopped. "So, what happened, boys?" she asked finally.

"Two of the big cousins were wrestling with each other back there," Peter said, "and Timmy was watching. He got all excited and jumped on top of them to help fight. One of the big boys jerked his head up, and it hit Timmy right in the nose!"

"Well, thank you for coming with him to find me," Mom told Peter. "Timmy," she said next, turning to her younger son, "I hope you have learned a lesson from this. It's dangerous to meddle, and stick your nose into trouble that is none of your business.

When you get involved in other people's fights, even though they may be just having fun, you are likely to get hurt. Being a peacemaker is good, but you must not try to help fight."

That evening after the visiting cousins had all gone home again, Mom talked with her boys some more.

"Proverbs seems to have a word of wisdom for every subject," she told them as she reached for her Bible. "And there is even a verse about what happened to Timmy today!" She paged through the book of Proverbs until she found the place she wanted. "See, boys? Proverbs 26:17 says: 'He that passeth by, and meddleth with strife belonging not to him, is like one that taketh a dog by the ears.'"

"'That taketh a dog by the ears'?" Peter repeated, laughing. "Whatever does *that* mean?"

"Well, suppose you would go up to a strange dog and grab hold of its ears," Mom explained. "What do you think would happen?"

"You would surely be bitten," Timmy replied soberly.

"That's right," Mom told him. "It would be a foolish thing to do. And this verse tells us that it's just as foolish to meddle with strife that is none of our business. Timmy, you found that out this afternoon! You thought it would be exciting to help with a fight, but you only got a bloody nose."

"The Bible also tells us a story about a king who made the same mistake," Mom went on, turning to a different place in her Bible. "King Josiah, in II Chronicles 36. Pharaoh Necho, the mighty king of Egypt, came up to fight against a city called Carchemish in a neighboring country. King Josiah of Judah had no reason to fight with Pharaoh Necho; but he decided to gather his army and go out against him.

"Pharaoh Necho sent ambassadors to Josiah, saying, 'What have I to do with thee, thou king of Judah? I come not against thee this day, but against a people whom God has told me to destroy. Now don't meddle with me, for God is on my side.'

"But king Josiah wanted to fight, and he would not listen. He came down into the valley of Megiddo with his little army, just like Timmy jumping onto the big boys. And Pharaoh Necho's archers shot at him with their arrows, so that he was sorely wounded. His servants quickly took him back to Jerusalem, and he died there. He learned too late how foolish it was to meddle with something that was none of his business.

"If you ever see other children fighting, boys," Mom told them, "and think that you know a way to help them make peace, you

131

should. But don't ever join in with fighting! It doesn't pay."

"Read us that verse about the dog's ears again, Mom," Timmy said softly.

So Mom turned back to Proverbs and read aloud once more, "'He that passeth by, and meddleth with strife belonging not to him, is like one that taketh a dog by the ears.'"

22

BOAST NOT OF TOMORROW

Proverbs 27:1, 2

"I'm going to beat!" Timmy shouted, leaping nimbly out of bed. His pajama top was already over his head and floating to the floor. "I'll beat all you slowpokes to get dressed this morning!"

"Aww, who cares," Peter replied, still snuggled under the covers. He was not usually so eager to get up in the morning as his younger brother.

"I'm going to beat! I'm going to beat!" Timmy sang tauntingly.

"Don't be so sure of that," Sharon called from the hallway. Looking up in surprise, Timmy saw that his big sister was not only dressed herself, but she was just pulling a dress over little Laura's head! Frantically, he yanked off his pajama bottoms and tugged on the blue pants hanging over his chair,

but Sharon had finished fastening the last button on Laura's dress before he even started with his shirt. "We beat you, Timmy!" Laura crowed.

Poor Timmy stood crestfallen and silent. "Ha, ha, Timmy!" Peter chuckled wisely as he swung his legs out of bed. "You shouldn't have bragged so loud."

"Well, anyway, I'm sure I'll beat *you*!" Timmy answered, brightening determinedly once more. He reached for his shirt. But, alas for Timmy -- on his first try he turned one shirt sleeve inside out. "No fair!" he wailed in frustration, struggling with the stubborn sleeve. Peter just laughed as he pulled his own clothes on. "See?" he said, buttoning his last shirt button and tucking the tail into his pants. "You didn't beat anybody! That's what you get for boasting."

Timmy pouted as he bumped slowly down the stairs. "Thump. Thump." his feet said on every step. He didn't feel like speaking to anyone.

Dad was sitting at the desk with his Bible open before him. He reached out a long arm to catch Timmy as he went by, and lifted him to his lap. "Timmy, Timmy," he said softly. "Are you sad so early in the morning?" Timmy turned his face against his father's shoulder and said nothing.

"You must learn that boasting is foolish and wrong, Timmy," Dad told him. The Bible says, right here in Proverbs, that we must not boast. It's foolish for us to brag of what we are going to do, because we never know how things will turn out.

"'Boast not thyself of the morrow,'" he read aloud, "'for thou knowest not what a day may bring forth.'

"If you hadn't been bragging so much this morning, Timmy, you wouldn't have needed to feel so disappointed now. And I'm sure the others would have been happy to help you when your shirt was inside-out, if only you hadn't boasted. It's silly to make such a fuss over who is first to get dressed."

"Breakfast is ready!" Mom called. The wonderful smell of pancakes floated in from the kitchen.

"Timmy, I was going to tell you a story of another boy who boasted," Dad said as he stood up. "But breakfast is ready, so I'll save the story for devotions tonight."

That evening the family turned to Proverbs 27, and the very first verse was: "Boast not thyself of the morrow, for thou knowest not what a day may bring forth. Let another man praise thee," Dad read on, "and not thine own mouth."

"Children, God's Word often tells us how the Lord hates pride and boasting," Dad told them. "And those attitudes are also disgusting to other people. Nobody likes to hear a person bragging about himself. We shouldn't

136

be proud of our abilities, because they are only blessings from God. And since we cannot know the future, it is foolish to boast of what we plan to do. So often our best plans get changed by things that happen.

"Whenever I read this verse about boasting, I remember something that happened when I was a boy not much older than Timmy. We were at a family reunion that day. I had tired of playing running games with the other small children, and was sitting on the grass by a group of older cousins, listening to their conversation. The young fellows were discussing what they planned to do when they were grown up, and I thought it was very interesting. One boy thought he would like to be a veterinarian, another wanted to go to Central America for voluntary service, and a third had ambitions of owning a fine cabinet shop.

"But big cousin Tom laughed at all the rest. 'You just wait and see,' he boasted. 'I'm going to be a rich man, with more money than any of you will ever have! I'm going to own at least three farms, with hired people to do all the work. Then I'll buy myself a private airplane and fly all over the country seeing all the sights! Yes, sir, I'm going to be a wealthy man!' Cousin Tom looked so confident and sure of himself! He leaned back in his chair and went on telling more about how he planned to be a millionaire.

"I grew tired of listening and ran off again, but I had heard enough to make an impression upon my little mind. Over the next few days I thought of Cousin Tom's words many times. 'Would I like to be rich too?' I wondered. But I didn't wonder for very long. Less than a week after that reunion day, my parents received a sad telephone call. Cousin Tom had been killed in a car accident.

"Big Cousin Tom, the one who had boasted about how rich he was going to be! Now his words would never come true. He had felt so sure of his future plans, but he had been so wrong.

"I never forgot what happened to Cousin Tom, and it has helped me remember not to boast. I learned at a young age that it's not wise to brag about our plans, since we never know what may happen. We do make plans, but we should always say, 'If the Lord is willing, we will.'

"So, children," Dad finished, "let's repeat the verse once again to help us remember."

"Boast not thyself of the morrow, for thou knowest not what a day may bring forth. Proverbs twenty-seven, one," the Millers recited in unison.

23

WHOSO CONFESSETH

Proverbs 28:13

The Miller family had a large, round glass fishbowl with seven goldfish. Timmy had received it for his birthday from Grandma Miller, and for nearly a year it had graced the top of Dad's filing cabinet near a living room window. This fish bowl, with its seven brightly colored occupants, was one of the children's favorite possessions! Everyone was eager to take his turn sprinkling in the daily pinch of fish food, and there was no lack of volunteers to help Mom clean the bowl and pebbles on Saturdays. Even though the goldfish had no names, they were family pets.

But one day, disaster threatened the goldfishes' peaceful home!

Laura was all alone in the living room, playing on the floor with the dollhouse Mom had made her from cardboard boxes. She hummed happily as she arranged her little "peoples" in their bedroom: the baby in his cradle, wrapped in a bit of fuzzy cloth, and the parents nearby. As Laura reached to the back of the little bedroom for another pile of tiny blankets, her hand bumped something hard and round. "Whatsis?" she muttered to herself. Grasping the object in her chubby fingers, she brought it out into the light. It was a marble, the big kind that Peter and Timmy didn't like because it became stuck in their marble roller.

"Dose big brothers!" Laura grumbled. "Dey shouldn't put dat in my people house!" And she flung the marble away with all the force in her small arm.

PLONK! The big marble struck the side of the glass fishbowl with an ominous thud. Startled, Laura whirled around. What had she hit? The sight she saw filled her with terror. Big cracks had appeared on the fishbowl, like the legs of a spider, fanning out from a small hole. A stream of water was slowly bubbling out, trickling down the side and spreading across the cabinet top!

Laura's heart pounded. Her knees felt weak and trembly! Panic seized her little mind, and she started crawling under the nearby coffee table to hide herself. What was going to happen now?

Peeking out from beneath the coffee table, Laura saw the trickle of water spreading and running down to the floor. The seven goldfish darted here and there, as if trying to escape the danger that threatened their lives. Laura's lips quivered, and tears began to flow as she crawled out of her hiding place. Crying loudly, she fled in search of her mother.

In the kitchen, Mom turned to pick up her crying daughter. "*What* did you do, Laura?" she asked, puzzled. "Fishbowl," Laura sobbed through her flood of tears. "It's broken and water dripping!"

Mom dropped the spoon she was holding and hurried to the living room. Instantly she saw the situation. Snatching up the dripping fishbowl, she dashed back to the kitchen and set it into the sink. Next she carefully poured the fish and their water into a bucket. "Daddy will probably be able to fix this hole," she told Laura. "But how did you ever make it?"

Laura was reluctant to tell. But finally the truth all came out, and Mom hugged her close. "Well, Laura," she said, "I hope this will help you remember not to throw toys. But I'm so glad you came and told me what had happened! If you had let all the water run out of the bowl, the goldfish would have died. Also, you would have been spanked for hiding what you had done instead of confessing. Since you came and told me the truth, I will not need to punish you."

That evening, the Millers discussed what had happened. Dad had patched the hole in the glass with silicon glue, and the bowl stood empty waiting to dry. "Tomorrow we should be able to put the fish back in, and hopefully they won't suffer any harm from their experience," Dad said. "We will always be able to see that patched place on the fishbowl, but I hope it will serve to remind us all of a very important truth."

"What truth is it, Dad?" Peter asked. "That we shouldn't throw marbles?" and he grinned at his little sister.

"Something even more important, Peter," Dad replied gravely. He opened his Bible to Proverbs 28 and began to read at the thirteenth verse: "He that covereth his sins shall not prosper, but whoso confesseth and forsaketh them shall find mercy."

"Here is another of the great laws of life," he explained to the family. "We all make mistakes sometimes, or commit sins, or break things. But if we try to cover up or hide what we have done, then the wrong becomes more serious. God wants people to confess their sins, and then they will find mercy. Laura confessed honestly to Mom what she had done, instead of trying to hide it. Since she told the truth, she was not punished for breaking the fishbowl.

"I'll tell you another little story, about myself when I was a boy," Dad went on. "One day I was with some neighbor boys when they decided to steal a few peaches out of an orchard nearby. I should never have given in to that temptation, nor gone with them! But I was very fond of fresh peaches, and I figured no one would ever know. That orchard had so many peaches, surely the owner wouldn't miss a few! So together we sneaked in through the back side of the orchard, darting behind trees whenever we heard a noise. Quickly we filled our hands and pockets, and dashed back to a safe place to eat the stolen fruit. Those peaches tasted good, and we were quite sure nobody had seen us!

"But God knew what we had done, and so did my conscience. Through the next days, as I went around trying to pretend that I had done nothing wrong, I was miserable. When it was time to pray, all I could think about was peaches. Whenever I sat down with a game or a book to read, it seemed as though peaches danced before my eyes. At night, when I closed my eyes and tried to go to sleep, all I could see was

144

those stolen peaches! All the time that I tried to cover up my sin, I did not prosper.

"My parents noticed that I was worrying about something, and one day Dad asked me what was wrong. I didn't like to tell him, but oh, what a relief I felt when the story finally came out! There was no need to hide my secret any longer.

"Dad spoke kindly to me. He could see that I had suffered enormous guilt over my wrongdoing. 'I will go with you to the neighbor's orchard,' he told me, 'and you can tell the owner what you did. You may pay him for the peaches you took, and then you will have peace again.'

"So that's just what we did. Dad took me to the orchard man's home, and I confessed to him about the stolen peaches. I gave him a few quarters to pay for them, but the man waved the money away. 'No, I don't need any money,' he told me cheerfully. 'I'm just glad to see you being honest. This will make a man out of you, boy!'

"So remember, children," Dad finished, "whoso confesseth and forsaketh his sin shall find mercy. Let's repeat that verse together."

"He that covereth his sins shall not prosper," the Millers recited, "but whoso confesseth and forsaketh them shall find mercy."

24

THE ROD AND REPROOF

Proverbs 29:15

One Saturday morning, Mom Miller was in the grocery store, and all four of the children were with her.

"This is fun!" Peter exclaimed. "I wish we could all go along for groceries more often! What shall I help you with, Mom?"

"Well, Peter, you may push the cart if you are careful," Mom replied with a smile. She lifted Laura into the seat in front of the cart. "Do you remember the time when you were little, and you tried to make the cart pop a wheelie?"

"I sure do," Peter answered, grinning with embarrassment. "I tipped the cart over on its end, and Timmy and Laura fell out. Laura was just a baby, too. I learned my lesson, never to do that again!" He gripped the handlebar of the cart firmly. "Don't worry, Laura," he told his sister. "I'll give you a nice, safe ride today."

"I wanna help too, Mom," Laura pleaded. "All right, you may carry the coupons," Mom told her. She sorted through her wallet and found the five coupons that she planned to use today.

"You hang onto those now, and don't drop any!" big sister Sharon warned the little girl. Timmy climbed into his place at the end of the cart, and the caravan of Millers began to roll down the aisle. "Sharon, you may get a big bag of those potatoes," Mom directed as she turned to choose a head of cabbage.

Just at that moment, a loud scream made all the Millers stop and look behind them. Back at the store entrance was a stout, red-faced woman trying to stuff her little girl, a child about Laura's size, into the seat of her cart. The little girl resisted with all her might, kicking and screaming, "No! NO! I wanna walk!"

The Millers turned back to their own shopping, but behind them they could hear the struggle continue, the strange little girl screaming and her mother shouting back. Abruptly the noise stopped. When Sharon looked around for a quick peek, she saw the cart coming down the aisle with the little girl skipping triumphantly alongside.

"Dat little girl is naughty," Laura whispered. "Shhh," Mom reproved quietly. She consulted her list as they turned into the next aisle.

"Timmy, reach down there and get one of those big cans of pork and beans," she told him. "We will need them for the school picnic." A tall stockman was unpacking a big box of bean cans, and Timmy needed to reach in front of him for the can Mom wanted. "Excuse me," he told the man softly.

"Of course, young fellow!" The stockman replied, cheerfully. "You're a real gentleman, aren't you? Not like some children," he added as the other cart behind the Millers turned the corner. The stout woman was trying to push her cart with one hand and drag her daughter with the other, and the little girl was shouting again. "I want chips!" she screamed. "I don't want those pretzels you got!"

Quietly the Miller family moved on. Peter pushed the cart with care, while Laura clutched Mom's little bundle of coupons. Sharon and Timmy helped Mom collect items from the shelves. When they came to the cereal aisle, Timmy looked longingly at the bright array of boxes. "Mom, couldn't we buy some of those red and yellow and purple cheerios?" he asked.

"Those are called Froot Loops," Peter said, reading the label. "Couldn't we try some, Mom?"

"No, boys, I'm sorry. Those are too sugary and too expensive," Mom replied. She reached for a box of plain cheerios, and another of cornflakes. The boys were disappointed, but they knew better than to argue.

When the family behind the Millers reached the cereal section, though, another noisy battle erupted. "No, I want this kind and that kind!" the little girl shrieked. "I want these, like they had on TV!" She snatched several boxes off the shelf, and when her mother tried to take them the little girl turned into a small whirlwind of fury. Kicking and waving her arms, she slammed into a cardboard display rack in the aisle! Boxes of cereal and fruit leather flew everywhere.

"Little brat, I'll kill you!" her mother screamed. A stock man hurried over. "Don't worry, lady, I'll pick everything up," he offered. Not bothering to thank him, the stout woman came fuming on down the aisle. "This child makes me so ashamed, I don't know why I ever take her along anywhere," she grumbled to Mom Miller as she passed. "Are your children always that good and quiet? I'd give this one away, if anyone would take her!" Without waiting for Mom to answer, she steamed off, dragging her little girl once more. The child turned to stare at the Millers as they passed. "Her eyes look so sad!" Sharon thought with a shiver.

When the Millers reached home, they were all eager to tell Dad about their shopping trip. "Dad, dere was a naughty little girl." Laura said, wide-eyed. "She kicked over a big pile of things in the store!" Timmy added, and the older children contributed more details to the story.

"Why do you think that little girl was so naughty, Dad?" Timmy asked. "Her mother must not be a Christian, and she probably never spanks her," Sharon put in wisely.

Dad picked up his two youngest and sat one on each of his knees. "Children, we can be very thankful for a Christian family," he told them soberly. "Your mother and I are trying to bring you up in the way that the Bible teaches, just like our parents brought us up. You could see today that God's way is the best and happiest way! That poor little girl in the grocery store is not happy, and neither is her mother. They are not following God's plan for parents and children.

"Remember yesterday's chapter of Proverbs?" Dad went on. "Verse 15 said this: 'The rod and reproof give wisdom, but a child left to himself bringeth his mother to shame.' That mother in the grocery store was brought to shame, because she had not trained her little girl properly. God's word says that the rod and reproof give wisdom. It's not fun to get a spanking, but sometimes it is necessary for learning wisdom. Parents and children who do not obey God's word will be brought to shame.

"Let's say Proverbs 29:15 all together," Dad told the children. "The rod and reproof give wisdom, but a child left to himself bringeth his mother to shame."

25

A WOMAN THAT FEARETH THE LORD

Proverbs 31:30

Sharon and her mother were having a quiet talk. Something was on Sharon's mind, so she had watched for a chance to catch Mom by herself. Now the two sat together at the kitchen table, and Sharon was able to tell her all about it.

"Mom, how can I have more friends?" she wondered. "I mean, I do have friends. But I wish I could be more like Mary Lou Raber. Everyone wants to be with Mary Lou, and do what she suggests. She always has something funny to say, and she's right in the middle of everything."

"You mean that Mary Lou is a popular girl?" Mom asked.

"Yes! popular is the right word," Sharon replied. She's so lively and exciting. And so pretty, too . . . " her voice trailed off.

Mom smiled rather sadly. "Sharon, I hope you are not seeking after the wrong kind of popularity," she told her daughter.

"What do you mean, Mom?"

"Well, Sharon, it is good to be kind and friendly to every one. A young girl should develop the skill of taking an interest in others, and making them feel happy and at ease with her. God does not want us to be aloof and self-centered. But popularity is a shallow and foolish thing, if it is based on prettiness, telling funny stories, or always trying to be the leader of a group."

Mom reached for her Bible, and turned to the last chapter of Proverbs. "Here, Sharon, is what we should desire to be," she said. "Verse 26: 'She openeth her mouth with wisdom, and in her tongue is the law of kindness.' Is Mary Lou always kind, Sharon, or do the funny things she says put others down?"

"I guess she does do that a lot," Sharon admitted. "Every one tries to stay on the good side of her, so she won't make fun of them."

"That doesn't sound like a skill you should want to imitate," Mom said softly. "Verse 30 says: 'Favor is deceitful, and beauty is vain: but a woman that feareth the Lord, she shall be praised.' Favor means charm or popularity, and the Bible tells us that it is deceitful! Sharon, I want to tell you a story of when I was a girl in the upper grades like you.

"There were a number of other girls in my class in those years, but I'm just going to tell you about two of them. Stephanie was a lively girl, very pretty and talkative, the popular type. She was like the queen bee: everyone wanted to be around her, to follow her lead and laugh at her stories. I knew Stephanie was not always kind, nor did she respect the teacher like she should have. But still I envied her. Even her name was so much more exciting than my plain ordinary name!

"Then there was Ida. Ida was a more serious-minded girl. She was not so pretty as Stephanie, and quiet by nature. She was always ready to help others, though, and knew the right things to do when anyone was hurt or in trouble. The little children in school loved her, and she often helped the lower grade teacher when her own work was done. Ida gave her heart to the Lord when we were in the seventh grade, and her life showed without any doubt that she was a true Christian! Some of the girls foolishly thought that she was too good.

"Ida was always kind and friendly, but she did not try to be the boss or get others to follow her. Stephanie acted in a silly way around the boys, trying for special attention from them, but Ida did not. She was always sensible. Even when children made fun of her name, calling her "Ida - hoe Potatoes", Ida just laughed along with them and did not get angry.

"My family moved away from that community when I was in the eighth grade, and I didn't get to finish the year with my friends there. In later years, though, I found out what had happened to my classmates as they grew up.

"Stephanie's story is not a happy one. When she was only sixteen, she ran away from her home and married a boy who was not a Christian. When I met her again years later, she was no longer lively or pretty. She was wearing worldly clothes and smoking a cigarrette, and I soon learned that she had been divorced from her husband. What a sad, lonely life Stephanie has now! Truly, favor was deceitful and beauty was vain, without the fear of the Lord!

"Ida is now a minister's wife, with a nice family of children. She is very happy, and she is admired and respected by everyone who knows her. Ida wisely chose the right path to follow, even as a young girl, and she has been rewarded for it. 'A woman that feareth the Lord, she shall be praised!'"

Sharon had listened soberly to her mother's story. "Do you think Mary Lou Raber will turn out to be like Stephanie?" she asked fearfully.

"I hope not," Mom answered. "Mary Lou has good parents who will try to guide her in the right way. But I hope she can be helped to see the folly of seeking after shallow popularity! Because the choices she makes now, and the habits she forms, will affect her life in years to come."

Sharon thought deeply that afternoon. The talk with her mother seemed to have opened up a new window for her to look through -- a window that made her look far out into her future. Sharon had always known that window would be there, and someday she would need to look through it. Someday she would need to decide for herself, to choose what kind of person she wanted to become. But was "someday" already here? Was Mom right when she said that her habits and choices *now* were making her into the woman she would be?

In the evening, the Millers gathered to read their last chapter of Proverbs. The circle of lamplight glowed warmly, and the children were very quiet as Dad read aloud.

"Who can find a virtuous woman? For her price is far above rubies . . . She stretcheth out her hand to the poor, yea, she reacheth out her hand to the needy . . . Strength and honour are her clothing, and she shall rejoice in time to come. She openeth her mouth with wisdom, and in her tongue is the law of kindness . . . Her children arise up, and call her blessed; her husband also, and he praiseth her. Many daughters have done virtuously, but thou excellest them all."

Dad paused, and turned to smile at his wife. A look of love passed between them, shining almost as brightly as the lamp itself, Sharon thought. "Many daughters have done virtuously, but thou excellest them all," Dad repeated tenderly. "Truly the Lord has blessed me, with a virtuous Christian wife!"

Sharon's breath caught in her throat. The view from that "window" was clear now! She no longer had any doubt which way she would choose. What was empty popularity worth, compared to the true honour and praise which a godly woman earned? "I will be wise like Ida -- and like Mother," Sharon decided, and peace filled her heart.

"Favour is deceitful and beauty is vain: but a woman that feareth the Lord, she shall be praised."

Also by Mildred A. Martin:
Storytime with the Millers
Valuable Lessons for children ages 4 - 8

Inquire at your favorite book dealer or write to:

Green Pastures Press
7102 Lynn Rd. N.E.
Minerva, OH 44657